BOOK OF METAPHORS
Volume II

Michael A. Gass, PhD

Association for Experiential Education

KENDALL/HUNT PUBLISHING COMPANY
4050 Westmark Drive   Dubuque, Iowa 52002

Cover illustration by Clint Metcalf and Jim Shreve.

♺ Printed on Recycled Paper

Copyright © 1995 by Association for Experiential Education

ISBN 0-7872-0306-8

Printed in the United States of America
10 9 8 7 6 5 4 3 2 1

CONTENTS

Foreword   *ix*

Dedication   *xiii*

Thoughts on Using Metaphors in Experiental Practices   **xv**

**Processing Adventure Experiences: Six Generations of
    Facilitating Adventure Experiences**   **1**

Designing Metaphoric Frames for Client Change   **11**

**The Ethics of Facilitation: Doing the Right Things with
    the Right People**   **19**

Therapeutic Populations   **25**
    Parents' Quality Call   27
    Family Strengths Protector   32
    Please Be Seated   35
    The Power Struggle (The Relationship Dance)   38
    Utilization Theory: Family Roles and the Blind Square   41
    The Trust Triangle: A Metaphor for Relationships   44
    Recovery Challenges   49
    The Wall and the Addiction Backpack   64
    Mohawk Traverse   67
    Sobriety Ball   69
    Mirk's Recovery   71
    Reentry   75
    Swing to Recovery (Disk Jockeys)   79
    A Road to Recovery: A Relapse Prevention Initiative   82

Recovery Activities   84
Getting Through Early Recovery: An Adaptable Metaphor   91
The Wild Woosey as a Way to Demonstrate Trust in a Method:
    A Metaphor for Acceptance of the AA Way   96
Funeral for a Friend   98
Celebrating Completion of "Group"   101
Vertigo: The Balance Broom as a Metaphor for the
    Natural Imbalance of Life   103
Utilization Theory: Desire for Change and the Wall   106
Tear Down the Wall   109
Creating "Personaphors" Through Personal
    Disclosure Activities   113
Climbing out of Shame   118
Window of Time   124
Life's a River   126
Standing Egg   130

Corporate Populations   **133**
The Meuse as a Metaphor for Business Operations in a
    Changing Environment   135
The Spider: A Measure of Quality   139
Blind Geometry and Teams Lacking Direction   142
Mineshaft or the Corporate Climb   145
Team Triangle   148
Computer Disinfectant   151
Refinery Re-Engineering   155
China Syndrome   159
Using "Target Specifications" for Business Populations 161
2B or Knot 2B   164
Corporate Ladder   167
The Bridge   171

School Populations   **173**
Team Ski   175
Goals, Barriers, and Resources   180
The Spider's Web as a Metaphor for Rules and Confronting
    Broken Rules   182

Toxic Waste Disposal: Active Listening Skills;
    Cooperative Group Effort   **184**
The Web of Academia   **187**
"ERTA": Estimated Relative Time Assessment   **190**
Membership Recruitment/Sorority Rush   **192**
The Practicum Web   **194**
Nurturing Family   **196**
Crossing the River of Knowledge   **198**
The Tension Traverse as a Metaphor for Problematic Group
     Dynamics in Individual Team Sports at the College Level   **201**
Rope Loops as a Metaphor for Change   **204**
Motivation Tag as a Metaphor for Giving and Receiving
     Positive Affirmations   **206**
The Communication Web: Active Listening Skills   **209**
Moon Ball as a Metaphor for Goal Setting   **212**

General Populations   **215**
Contemplation Exercises for Active, Creative Thinking   **217**
Visiting a Seniors' Home   **221**
The Chocolate Game   **225**

List of Activities   **230**

List of Contributors   **231**

List of Karl Rohnke's Books   **232**

Additional Books From AEE   **233**

ABOUT THE ASSOCIATION FOR EXPERIENTIAL EDUCATION

The Association for Experiential Education (AEE) is a not-for-profit, international, professional organization committed to furthering experiential-based teaching and learning in a culture that is increasingly "information-rich but experience-poor." By allowing the student, client, or customer to be involved in decisions about what they need to learn, and how they might go about learning, we believe lifelong learning is the result.

AEE sponsors local, regional, and international conferences, projects, seminars, and institutes and publishes the *Journal of Experiential Education*, the *Jobs Clearinghouse*, directories of programs and services, and a wide variety of books and periodicals to support educators, trainers, practitioners, students, and advocates.

AEE's diverse membership consists of individuals and organizations with affiliations in education, recreation, outdoor adventure programming, mental health, youth service, physical education, management development training, corrections, programming for people with disabilities, and environmental education.

To receive additional information about the Association for Experiential Education, call or write: AEE, 2885 Aurora Avenue #28, Boulder, CO, 80303–2252, USA. (303) 440–8844, (303) 440–9581 (FAX)

ABOUT THE THERAPEUTIC ADVENTURE PROFESSIONAL GROUP (TAPG)

The Therapeutic Adventure Professional Group is committed to the development and promotion of experiential education in therapeutic settings. We are also committed to the professional development of our members and the profession as a whole.

Therapeutic Adventure is the professional group for those AEE members who use experiential education therapeutically within the fields of health, mental health, corrections, education, and other human service fields. Our primary mission is the networking of professionals within our various fields and the sharing of information, techniques, and concerns regarding the therapeutic use of experiential education. We define therapeutic as moving toward healthy change. Additionally, we seek to represent the interests of our membership to the Board and larger professional communities through newsletters, publications, articles, workshops, and pre-conference activities.

FOREWORD

"What goes around, comes around.
And here we go again."

The premise for this book began on a long bike ride I was taking with Craig Dobkin in the summer of 1989. During this time, we found ourselves invested in one of those wonderfully productive conversations that often occur during such experiences. Our discussion centered around the importance of how experiences are presented to achieve their educational or therapeutic objectives. It became particularly evident to us (as we're sure that it has to other professionals) that our field does a good job of writing and letting others know how to conduct adventure experiences (e.g., Karl Rohnke's work), but we really are delinquent in sharing how we prepare experiences, particularly metaphorical ones, with other professionals.

Based on that idea, we emerged from the ride with the intention to compile a "Book of Metaphors" focusing on such presentations. Our method for accomplishing this task was simply this: If people were willing to take the time to share their ideas on how they "framed" or structured an experience, we would be willing to put all these ideas together and send them back to the contributors. We hoped people would see the value in this type of professional reciprocity and respond to our call for contributions.

We presented this idea at the 1989 AEE Conference in Santa Fe, New Mexico. The response to our task was wonderful in both quality and number. Within two years we received over 55 contributions from 45 authors. One piece that was extremely enriching was work done by Stephen Barcia Bacon for Outward Bound in a one-time publication called the *Curriculum Newsletter*. To us, all of the people who contributed to the book personified the highest level of professional service: individuals investing time and effort in others to make professional interventions with clients more meaningful and enriching. We have found it to be actions like these that move the field in its most positive directions.

With the publication of the first book in 1991, there was also an increasing professional investment in the use of proactive framing techniques. Professionals like Lee Gillis, Simon Priest, Jackie Gerstein, Cindy

Clapp, Relly Nadler, Marianne Scippa, Scott Banderhoff, Christian Itin, Eileen Morris, Peter Naitove, Betsy Hearn, Martin Ringer, Juli Lynch, and others were furthering the profession's vision on the prescriptive use of direct and indirect methods of facilitating functional change. With this growth, I also saw a chance to create some "system" where the spirit of what others had contributed would continue. Based on this premise, we chose not to sell the book, but instead to provide a copy to those who contributed one of their pieces of work to create Volume II. This process also included offering several workshops throughout North America on these facilitation styles in an attempt to help others nurture their ideas even further. This work has produced the second collection that lies before you. Combined with this collection is a brief series of my thoughts on facilitation styles, a method for framing experiences, and the ethics of facilitating client experiences.

The "fallout" of this system has produced even further benefits. One is that the field is exposed to a broader network of individuals doing meaningful work, individuals who continue the ethic of service that furthers the profession in its best directions. The second is that all of the proceeds from this book are donated in an unrestricted manner to the Association for Experiential Education (AEE) and the Therapeutic Adventure Professional Group (TAPG) to further their objectives.

What about receiving a copy of Volume I? It would be wonderful to see the growth of a third edition, and in the spirit that created this second volume, the same offer for receiving Volume I stands. Send a copy of an activity and the manner in which you facilitate it to Michael A. Gass, Book of Metaphors, NH Hall, 124 Main Street, UNH, Durham, NH 03824, USA. By doing this you receive a copy of Volume I, aid in the development of the third volume, and add to the richness of what the field is accomplishing. If possible, follow the format that exists in this book to make it more readily useable for others. This format consists of the following seven sections:

1. *Title*—Use a title for the learning experience that mirrors the population and resulting change of the activity.
2. *Introduction*—Describe the population this experience is designed for, when it might be used in a progression (in the beginning as an assessment activity, as an intervention, for the termination of the group, etc.), what some contraindicating or limiting factors might be, and any other pertinent information.
3. *Goals*—Describe the goals that this activity reaches. Rank them in order of importance if possible.
4. *Set-up*—Describe the logistical set-up needed for the activity, including safety (e.g., emotional, physical) considerations.

5. *Sample presentation*—In language that is appropriate (e.g., respectful, appropriate intellectual level) for the client, write out
   the "frame" or presentation you would use as a facilitator to
   enhance the client's experience.
6. *Logistics*—Describe those things that you would do as a facilitator
   during the activity to enhance the value of the experience.
7. *Debriefing*—Emphasize those issues that occurred during the
   activity, being especially sensitive to clients' past behaviors,
   current needs, and future considerations.
8. *Your name, address, and phone number*—Include this so other
   interested professionals can contact you and celebrate your work!

Again, send this to: Michael A. Gass, Book of Metaphors, NH Hall, 124
Main Street, UNH, Durham, NH 03824, USA. Call (603) 862-2024 if you
have questions. If writing is difficult for you, several alternative methods
exist for us to transmit your wonderful ideas to others.

Thanks again for your professional spirit and your support of the
Association for Experiential Education. Welcome to the work of some very
special people; I encourage you to contact them at the addresses that are
provided at the end of each presentation. We will all be richer for the
interaction.

Michael A. Gass
September 20, 1994

DEDICATION
(as well as a metaphor
for clients and facilitators)

This book is dedicated
To children, including the ones inside all of us,
for they know the importance of stories
and which ones are the best,

and

To the times when parents decide to tell the best stories
and when they decide to remain silent and let them occur.

THOUGHTS ON USING METAPHORS IN EXPERIENTIAL PRACTICES

A single word
can possess multiple meanings;
yet as the common saying goes,
one picture can be worth a thousand words.

And if a picture
can be worth a thousand words,
then one experience
can be worth a thousand pictures;

And if an experience
can be worth a thousand pictures,
then one metaphor
can be worth a thousand experiences.

But in the end,
a metaphor possesses value only when:

- *it is able to interpret the right experience*
- *in a manner that provides the right picture*
- *that produces the right words*
- *that have deep meaning*
- *for that particular person.*

PROCESSING ADVENTURE EXPERIENCES: SIX GENERATIONS OF FACILITATING ADVENTURE EXPERIENCES[1]

If you always do
what you've always done,
you'll always get
what you've always got.
If what you're doing is not working,
do something else.

—Craig Dobkin & other authors

The evolution of facilitating adventure experiences has passed through several distinct stages of development (e.g., Bacon, 1987; Doughty, 1991; Priest & Gass, 1993). Emerging out of this evaluating process have been several different styles of facilitation, with earlier forms fostering the growth of more recent styles. Each of these styles can be categorized, in order of occurrence and sophistication, as follows:

1. Letting the experience speak for itself
2. Speaking for the experience
3. Debriefing the experience

4. Directly frontloading the experience
5. Framing the experience
6. Indirectly frontloading the experience

Note the line differentiating the first three forms of facilitation from the last three styles. This line represents a philosophical shift in the

1. The foundation of these thoughts can be found in: Priest, S. & Gass, M. A. (1993). Five generations of facilitated learning from adventure education. *Journal of Adventure Education and Outdoor Leadership, 10*(3), 23–25.

approach facilitators take in processing adventure experiences. In each of these latter styles, a major focus has been placed on the use of proactive techniques to respectfully enhance a client's adventure experience and its future applications. Such techniques are not utilized in the first three styles.

Besides the existence of these proactive techniques, it is also important to note where the latter three styles center their focus on changing behavior. All three of these styles are heavily influenced by the belief that the strength of changing behavior is affected more by the actual experience than by the analogies created by reflective techniques conducted after the experience (e.g., debriefing). These latter styles represent the majority of experiences and frameworks presented in this book.

THE SIX GENERATIONS

The six generations of facilitation, and some of their strengths and weaknesses, may be summarized as follows:

Letting the Experience Speak for Itself

"Letting the experience speak for itself" is a method found in numerous adventure programs where the facilitation associated with programming consists of providing well-planned experiences and leaving clients to sort out their own personal understandings (Doughty, 1991). When properly sequenced and well designed, the inherently enriching qualities of adventure experiences are meant to lead clients to their own insights (i.e., "learning by doing only"). This approach is fine, provided that identified or prescriptive intrapersonal and interpersonal goals are not sought. Clients are likely to have a good time and possibly become proficient at an adventure skill, but they may be less likely to have learned anything about themselves, how they relate with others, or how to resolve certain issues confronting them in their lives.

Speaking for the Experience

In an effort to enhance programming efforts, some programs have implemented the second generational approach of "speaking for the experience." Here the facilitator (often in the role of a consultant or expert) interprets the experience on behalf of the clients, informing them of what they learned and how they should apply their new knowledge in the future. This second approach of "learning by telling" may be well suited for role plays and simulations where results are predictable and reproducible. In adventure experiences, however, group members tend to present unique behavioral traits from the way they act under stress. The results from these experiences also seem to be more unpredictable, unique, and varied than those found in some other learning environments. Telling clients what they received from an experience may also be disempowering, hamper future opportunities for growth, and alienate the facilitator from clients.

Debriefing the Experience

The solution to such facilitation problems has been to encourage "learning through reflection" or debriefing approaches.

As clients bring up issues or state personal commitments to change, they are more likely to personalize and follow through on changes if they possess ownership over such issues. This idea, popularized in North America as the "Outward Bound Plus" model (Bacon, 1987), has given rise to the third generational approach of "debriefing" experiences. Here, clients are asked to reflect on adventure experiences and discuss points of learning they believe took place. These processes are usually initiated by facilitators carefully designing questions and guiding clients to discover their own learnings. Some successful examples of debriefing approaches include the "Funnelling" approach (Priest & Naismith, 1993), portions of the "Adventure Wave Plan" (Schoel, Prouty, & Radcliffe, 1988), and other methods based on progressive learning (e.g., Quinsland & Van Ginkel, 1984; Hammel, 1986).

Directly Frontloading the Experience

While the reflection processes identified above are typically accomplished after the experience, a number of facilitators have concluded there may be some added benefit by directing the clients before the experience even begins. This type of thinking has led to the fourth generation approach of directly frontloading the experience, adding an emphasis on an extra "prebriefing" beyond the usual statements concerning safety, logistics, etc. prior to the experience. In the third stage, it is quite common for facilitators to brief clients before the experience by explaining how the activity should work and then debrief clients afterwards on the applications of learning through guided inquiry and reflective discussions. In the fourth stage, however, additional "frontloading" is held prior to engaging in the adventure as the instructor highlights several key points. These points may address one or more of the following five topics:

a. *Revisit*—"What was learned in the last activity and how can we apply these ideas in the next activity?"

b. *Objectives*—"What do you think are the objectives of this activity and what can be learned or gained from this experience?"

c. *Motivation*—"Why do you think experiencing the activity might be important in how it relates to our daily lives?"

d. *Function*—"What behaviors do you think will help bring about our success and how can we optimize these?"

e. *Dysfunction*—"What behaviors do you think will hinder our success and how can we overcome these barriers?"

In essence, clients are directed toward certain distinct objectives assessed by the facilitator based on their needs. By emphasizing key issues up front, debriefing becomes a reemphasis of learnings rather than a reactive discussion as seen in the third generation models.

Framing the Experience

The fifth generation of facilitation, still relatively uncommon in adventure programming, involves framing experiences isomorphically. Isomorphs are parallel structures proactively introduced by the facilitator so clients can make relevant metaphoric connections prior to the activity. When these connections are motivating and relevant to the client, the transfer of learning is usually enhanced. These isomorphic connections are created by the facilitator "framing" the adventure experience to serve as a mirror image of the client's reality. As with direct frontloading, only a relatively small amount of debriefing is needed after the experience, becoming more of a "reinforcement in reflection," as learners discuss the close connections between the adventure experience and their "everyday" lives. Framing experiences may be more appropriate in therapeutic or training and development programs, where specific prescriptive changes may be the intent, rather than in some educational adventure programs that possess more general ‚focuses.

Indirectly Frontloading the Experience

Even more rare than the fifth generation of facilitation are instances involving the use of indirect approaches to frontloading client experiences. This usually arises when the facilitator finds clients with continuing problematic issues. Common examples of problematic issues are when: (1) The harder the client tries to eliminate the unwanted issue, the more it occurs, or (2) the more a client tries to attain a desired result, the more elusive this result becomes. Several forms of indirect frontloading include: (1) double binds, (2) symptom prescriptions, (3) symptom displacements, (4) illusion of alternatives, and (5) proactive reframing (e.g., Waltzlawick, 1978).

SIX EXAMPLES

The following illustration of a well-known adventure experience (i.e., the Spider's Web) is used to illustrate each of the formats in the six-stage generational model explained above. The differences in facilitation exemplify the characteristics of each style.

In *"letting the experience speak for itself,"* the facilitator would not look to add any insights regarding the Spider's Web exercise when the experience was completed. If any comments were made, they might pertain to how much fun the experience was and encourage the group to move on and try the next event (e.g., *"That was great! Good job! Now let's try something else."*).

In *"speaking for the experience,"* the facilitator would provide the group with feedback about their general behaviors after the activity was completed (e.g., what they did well, what they need to work on, and what they learned from the exercise). Examples of such statements might include: *"You've learned to cooperate by virtue of working together and succeeding. Your communication is poor, everyone is talking, and no one seems to be listening to anyone's ideas. The level of trust seems to be improving, since no one appeared to worry about being picked up by the others. It seems you could have benefited from having a leader or coordinator for this activity!"*

In *"debriefing the experience,"* the facilitator would foster a group discussion concerning the details, analysis, and evaluation of the group's behavior following the activity completion. Sample questions of this facilitational style might include: *"What happened? What was the impact of this? How did that make you feel? What did you learn from this? What aspects for this activity were metaphors of your life?* and *What will you do differently next time?"*

With directly *"frontloading the experience,"* the facilitator would introduce the Spider's Web with the same logistical briefing as usual (e.g., group members must be passed through the opening in the web, from this side to that one, without touching the strands. Contact with a strand wakes the spider, which bites you and causes you to start over. A repeat contact sends your whole group back to the beginning). In addition to this, the facilitator may add a series of questions to focus the learning prior to the activity *(e.g., "What do you think this exercise might teach you? Why is learning this important? How might your learning help you in the future? Do you recall from past exercises what each of you wanted to work on in situations like this?")*. Since this frontloaded pre-briefing has already covered many of the topics usually held in debrief, the concluding discussion can concentrate on summarizing what answers were discovered for this question.

In *"framing the experience,"* the facilitator would provide a pre-briefing in terms of the similar structures between the adventure and corresponding present life experiences of the participant. For example, with a group working in a company warehouse, the Spider's Web might be introduced as a distribution network (the web) through which goods and services (team members) are passed from the warehouse (one side) to the customer's many outlets (other side). Passage takes place along unique routings (openings) and contact with the network (brushing up against a strand) damages the goods and services, which means they need to be returned to the warehouse. If damaged goods and services are purposely passed on to the customer, then all shipments will be refused by the customer and returned to the warehouse to be fixed and shipped again! If this form of briefing is close to a mirror image of the workplace and current reality of this organization, then the debrief generally focuses on punctuating the learnings acquired in the experience.

With *"indirect frontloading,"* the facilitator may present an introduction to a problematic group with sexist behaviors as follows:

> *Most corporate groups who attempt the Spider's Web tend to do it in a particular way. At the beginning, they mill around a bit with lots of people offering their suggestions. After some time, a couple of dominant males tend to start the group off. They get a few men to the other side of the Spider's Web, and then throw the women through like sacks of potatoes, and often with embarrassing remarks about their personal anatomy. Then the same group of dominant males decides how to do the hardest part of the task, which is getting the last*

few people through. Afterwards, during the discussion of the exercise, everyone agrees that the leadership was more or less sexist and there are various emotional reactions. There are other ways to do the Spider's Web. Other groups have found them and I hope this group does too (Adapted from Bacon, 1993).

Stated in this way with this particular group, this "double bind" creates a "win-win" situation. If the group chooses to perform the task in a sexist manner, then they "win" because their true behaviors will become painfully obvious and the awareness or denial of the group's sexist behavior will be heightened for the debriefing. If the group chooses to perform in a non-sexist and equitable manner, then they also "win" since they have clearly demonstrated they can act differently and may continue to do so in the future. One way brings dysfunction to the forefront of discussion, while the other breaks old habits and provides new learning. With this technique, the facilitator has "bound" this resistant client group in a functional manner to a unique learning opportunity.

CONCLUSIONS

Each of these facilitation styles holds particular meaning for certain clients using adventure experiences for specific reasons. Adventure organizations using any of these facilitation styles have a responsibility to consider what style is most appropriate, based on client needs as well as staff abilities.

Note that there can be several drawbacks to using the more sophisticated styles of processing. Some of these may include:

1. These approaches are more complex than other facilitation styles. In addition to all the other tasks associated with facilitation (e.g., needs assessment, design, delivery, debriefing, follow-up, safety, and ethics), proper structuring and framing of tasks add additional responsibility to conducting the experience. Failure to attend to these details can result in negative consequences for clients.

2. When using these styles, facilitators need to be more prescriptive in their techniques. This often requires a greater breadth and depth of assessment concerning the needs of clients, as well as an understanding of what change will mean to a client's future. Without this information, certain styles can be inappropriate as well as unable to assist clients in producing lasting change in their lives.

3. The efficacy of these approaches depends upon the ability of clients to perceive (at one level or another) parallel structures. Metaphors and isomorphs can be confusing things to the uninitiated. Confusion can easily lead to clients missing the isomorphic connections of the experience.

4. Presenting isomorphic frameworks also requires an ability on the part of the facilitator to match their introduction to the client's reality. Knowledge of a client's language and other symbols is important, but facilitators should not underestimate the importance of properly comprehending the client's reality. Truly effective framing requires much more than merely placing labels or images from the client's environment onto adventure experiences.

5. No two members of a group are alike and facilitators must account for the individual differences among clients when working with groups. Creating frames that are open enough for each client to internalize their own personal perspectives will lead to a greater ability to produce individual change. Failure to do this (presenting closed or restrictive frames) may limit individual as well as group development.

6. By narrowing the focus of a frame to a predetermined metaphoric message, the facilitator is emphasizing what will be learned in the activity. Even if the facilitator is correct with the frame, prescribing certain frameworks may limit the interpretation of other frameworks by clients. Since the transfer of learning can be closely linked to metaphoric connections, loss of meaningful metaphors for some people may inhibit the future relevance for clients.

REFERENCES

Bacon, S. B. (1987). *The evolution of the Outward Bound process.* Greenwich, CT: Outward Bound, USA. (ERIC Document Reproduction Service No. ED 295 780)

Bacon, S. B. (1991). Sex role stereotyping and the wall. In M. A. Gass and C. Dobkin, *Book of Metaphors, Volume I*. University of New Hampshire.

Bacon, S. B. (1993). Paradox and double binds in adventure-based education. In M. A. Gass (Ed.), *Adventure therapy: Therapeutic applications of adventure programming.* Dubuque, IA: Kendall-Hunt Publishing Company.

Doughty, S. (1991). Three generations of development training. *Journal of Adventure Education and Outdoor Leadership*, 7(4), 7–9.

Gass, M. A. (1991). Enhancing metaphoric transfer in adventure therapy programs. *Journal of Experiential Education, 14*(2), 6–13.

Gass, M. A. & Priest, S. (1993). Using metaphors and isomorphs to transfer learning in adventure education. *Journal of Adventure Education and Outdoor Leadership.*

Hammel, H. (1986). How to design a debriefing session. *Journal of Experiential Education, 9*(3), 20–25.

Priest, S. & Naismith, M. (1993). The debriefing funnel. *Journal of Adventure Education and Outdoor Leadership, 10*(3), 20–22.

Quinsland, L. K. & Van Ginkle, A. (1984). How to process experience. *Journal of Experiential Education, 7*(2), 8–13.

Waltzlawick, P. (1978). *The language of change.* New York: W. W. Norton & Company.

DESIGNING METAPHORIC FRAMES FOR CLIENT CHANGE

In the end
we conserve
only what we love;

we will love only
what we understand;

and we will understand
only what we are taught

—Baba Dioum (Senegal)

The use of metaphors to create change can occur before, during, or after experiences.[1] One model that has been created to assist in the development of pre-experience metaphors (i.e., framing) is a seven-step process outlined by Gass (1993). The steps in this model include:

1. *State and rank goals*—State and rank the specific and focused goals of the therapeutic intervention based on the assessment of the client's needs. Without knowledge of what the client's issues are and how they affect them, it is difficult to construct a solution-oriented metaphor that will assist them.
2. *Select metaphoric adventure experience*—Select an adventure experience that possesses a strong metaphoric relationship to the goals of therapy.

---

1. For further references and readings in the area of adventure therapy, the reader is encouraged to explore the following resources: Bacon & Kimball (1989); Gass (1993); Gillis & Bonney (1986); Schoel, Prouty, & Radcliffe (1986); and Tobler (1986).

3. *Identify successful resolution to the therapeutic issue*—Show
   how the experience will have a different successful ending/
   resolution from the corresponding real life experience.
4. *Strengthen isomorphic framework*—Adapt the framework (e.g.,
   title introduction, rules, process) of the adventure experience so
   that it becomes even more metaphoric and the participant can
   develop associations to the concepts and complexity of the
   experience. Make sure that the connections creating the metaphoric process (i.e., isomorphs) possess the appropriate content
   and relationships between one another.
5. *Review client motivation*—Double check to make sure that the
   structured metaphor is compelling enough to hold the
   individual's attention without being too overwhelming.
6. *Conduct experience with revisions*—Conduct adventure experience, making adjustments to highlight isomorphic connections
   (e.g., appropriate reframing).
7. *Debrief*—Use debriefing techniques following the experience
   to reinforce positive behavior changes, reframe potentially
   negative interpretations of the experience, and focus on the
   integration of functional change into the client's lifestyle.

The following description is one example of how an adventure
experience can be structured using this model to create functional
change for clients participating in a substance abuse program. The
issues of this particular group were: (1) the ability to ask for help, (2)
the ability to set appropriate boundaries around issues of recovery to
maintain abstinence, and (3) the elimination of dysfunctional behaviors
that undermine the ability to maintain abstinence (e.g., placing the
needs of others ahead of the need to stay sober).

Figure 1 illustrates how the planning of this initiative used each of
these seven steps to reach its treatment objective.

Note that this activity (i.e., the Maze) is constructed by connecting
rope in and around a group of trees at the waist level of participants (see
Rohnke, 1989, pp. 103–104).[2] The usual objective is for individuals

---

2. It is important to recognize that as initiatives/ropes course elements are adapted
   for specific educational or therapeutic uses, the field must not forget the debt it
   owes to the originators of these activities (e.g., Rohnke, 1989) who made such
   powerful mediums possible. These activities are not adapted to minimize the
   creative work these pioneers have accomplished, but to build even greater
   bridges for educational and therapeutic change. (References to Karl Rohnke's
   work are found throughout this book; a list of the books mentioned can be
   found on page 232 .)

FIGURE 1

Application of the seven-step process for creating metaphoric transfer
to the Path to Recovery activity

---

1. State
   and rank
   goals

   a. Ability to ask for
      help
   b. Set healthy bound-
      aries around
      recovery issues
   c. Eliminate specific
      dysfunctional
      behaviors (e.g.,
      rescuing, enabling)

2. Select
   isomorphic
   experience

   The Maze activity
   (Rohnke, 1989)

3. Identify
   successful
   resolution
   to the
   therapeutic
   issues

   a. Asking for
      assistance
   b. Choosing behav-
      iors that place ab-
      stinence first
   c. Avoiding rescuing
      and enabling
      behaviors

4. Strengthen
   isomorphic
   framework

   a. Create description
      that is analogous to
      the current state
      and needs of client
   b. Make exit from
      maze dependent
      upon each person's
      ability to ask for
      help
   c. Revise choice
      decision to mirror
      client's choice of
      abstinence or
      continual "blind-
      ing"
      addiction process
   d. Make choice
      decision mirror
      negative conse-
      quences of rescu-
      ing or enabling
      behaviors

   e. Create abstinence
      area where clients
      can still be present
      near individuals
      "using"
   f. Create other rel-
      evant analogies

5. Review
   client
   motivation

   a. Use an appropriate
      progression of
      activities that lead
      up to this activity
   b. Review level of
      group development
   c. Ensure clients feel
      relatively comfort-
      able when blind-
      folded
   d. Review verbal
      framework to en-
      sure its isomorphic
      connection between
      adventure experi-
      ence and treatment
      objectives

6. Conduct
   experience
   revisions

   a. Make necessary
      safety with
      adjustments
   b. Provide appropriate
      reframing

7. Debrief

   a. Center discussion
      around treatment
      objectives
   b. Use debriefing to
      picture isomorphic
      connections

(while blindfolded) to make their way out of this maze by holding onto the rope, following it from tree to tree, and finding a pre-determined exit established by the facilitator.

In working with the clients possessing these substance abuse issues, the physical structure of the activity remains the same, yet the title, introduction, logistics, framework, and associated debriefing of the initiative are changed to create stronger connections (i.e., isomorphs) to these issues.[3] One example of a pre-activity introduction that used this activity for this particular client group proceeded in the following manner (Note: participants put their blindfolds on prior to this description):

> *The next activity is called the Path to Recovery. It's called that because a number of the obstacles you'll encounter are very similar to obstacles many of you are currently encountering in your addictions. Our addictions often blind us in our path to a substance-free lifestyle, and we often fail because we don't remember to live by principles that will allow us to free ourselves from abusive substances.*
>
> *After my description of this activity, I will place you on the road to recovery by putting your hand on a rope. This rope leads you along a path of indeterminable length. Along your journey to recovery, you will meet a variety of other people going in different directions. Some of these people will be in a great hurry, showing a lot of confidence. Others will be tentative, moving cautiously. Some will seem to know the right direction, whereas others will seem lost. Don't let go of the rope, because if you do you will lose the path and we will have to ask you to sit down until the initiative is over.*
>
> *The goal of your journey is to reach one of the exits to abstinence. There are several exits in this maze, and as you reach one of these exits, I'll be there to ask you an important choice. The choice will be: (1) whether you wish to choose to step out of the maze—if you make this decision, I'll ask you*

---

3. This activity is used most appropriately after a series of progressive activities that allow participants to look at such powerful issues in a safe manner. For example, it should be used with groups who have: (1) worked together for an appropriate period of time, (2) already established a sense of group identity, (3) members that can feel relatively comfortable and safe when blindfolded, and (4) experienced previous adventure experiences involving issues of trust, support, risk, and challenge. To introduce an initiative with this much confrontation to unprepared clients would contraindicate treatment and be unethical.

to remove your blindfold and sit quietly in the abstinence area until this initiative is over—or (2) you may choose to go back into the maze to help others. If you choose to go back into the maze, you run the risk that this particular exit may be shut when you return and you will have to find another exit.

If at any time during this activity you would like to receive help, all you need to do is ask for it and guidance will be provided. Otherwise we would like everyone not to speak throughout this initiative until it is completed.

Remember the rules of the initiative:
- *Follow the safety rules we've provided.*
- *No speaking unless you want help.*
- *I will be waiting for you at the exit of the maze and ask you to make your decision.*

After approximately 30 minutes, I will ask those of you still in the maze to remove your blindfolds for a small break.

After delivering this introduction, instructors distribute clients throughout the maze and tell them not to move until the go-ahead is given. When all of the clients have been placed in the maze, they are told to search for an exit. In this initiative, however, the exits remain closed until each person asks for help. The exit only opens up for the person asking for help.

After clients ask for help, they are informed that they have created a pathway from their addictive process and that they are ready to make an important decision for themselves. If clients choose to step out, they are asked to remove their blindfolds and step aside to observe others in the maze in a designated abstinence area. It is important for these clients to remain in the abstinence area and silently observe the rest of the process. If clients choose to go back into the maze, their blindfold remains on and their exit closes and remains closed until they ask for help again. If clients become grouped near an exit, each person is informed that they must make their own decision independently from others.

The initiative is usually stopped after 30 minutes even though some clients may still be in the maze, usually because they keep going back in to rescue others. At this point, the clients still in the maze are asked to quietly remove their blindfolds and come and join the rest of the group in a circle.

ANALYSIS OF THE EXPERIENCE

Different issues can arise within each group during the debriefing. In this case the facilitator began the process by asking people to relate their experience in the initiative to their experience in trying to reach or maintain sobriety. Given the treatment orientation and objectives, discussions have generally focused around: (1) how asking for help assisted people in this initiative, (2) people's choices at the exits, and (3) what "failing to hold on" to the rope represented.

In the beginning of the debriefing, clients are informed that the exits weren't opened until someone asked for help. The clients that called for help are asked to describe how this assisted them in finding their exit. They are also asked to elaborate on why they asked for help and what it felt like to receive assistance. The objective of including this dynamic in the initiative is to enhance the isomorph of people with substance abuse issues asking for help, particularly when feeling lost or "blinded" by their addictions.

The "choice" decision is meant to be isomorphic with a critical boundary issue for these clients, since their recovery process must be considered first in any decision. Stepping out of the maze is isomorphic to a healthy personal decision. Choosing to go back in is isomorphic to a dangerous decision, one where they may never have the opportunity to achieve an exit to abstinence again.

Sometimes people (e.g., adolescents) state that they stayed in the maze because "stepping out" would be "boring." This is a key issue to emphasize in the debriefing since abstinence may seem less exciting than "being in the game." This "exciting" game, however, possesses tragic consequences for many substance abusers. Some other important metaphors to discuss may include:

■ To "let go" of the rope is to lose a chance to achieve abstinence.
■ The feelings of abstainers observing others "lost" in the maze of abusive substances.
■ Metaphorical techniques participants used to "find an exit" to abstinence (e.g., the struggle of "searching").
■ Interaction with others searching for abstinence in the maze.
■ The inability to communicate while searching for abstinence.
■ The role of hospitals/treatment centers in "placing" clients on the road to abstinence and the role of the client following the path and making choices.

It is important to note that the goals for this particular population are isomorphic for clients focusing on the first and second steps of the AA process (e.g., Alcoholics Anonymous, 1976). If the needs of clients are different (e.g., focusing on ninth or 12th step issues), the initiative should be structured differently. Therapists with other orientations or theoretical structures for treating substance issues would obviously frame their isomorphs differently based on the treatment objectives. It is critical for therapists using this technique to be clear on the objectives of therapy, or the use of therapeutic adventure experiences becomes a "hit or miss" strategy for intervention.

It is also important to note that the creation of therapeutic isomorphs can also vary based on the characteristics of the therapeutic population. This example has been used successfully with a variety of client groups, including adolescents as well as adults, men and women, and clients from African-American, Anglo, or Chicano cultures. Individuals possessing various interpretive frameworks require different therapeutic introductions and adventure experiences to produce equally beneficial results. Just as it is important for facilitators to tailor experiences to specific therapeutic goals, it is equally important to consider each client's background in the assessment and prescription of therapeutic interventions.

REFERENCES

Alcoholics anonymous. (1976). New York: Alcoholics Anonymous World Services, Inc.

Bacon, S. (1983). *The conscious use of metaphor in Outward Bound.* Denver, CO: Colorado Outward Bound School.

Gass, M. A. (1991). *Adventure therapy: Therapeutic applications of adventure programming.* Dubuque, IA: Kendall Hunt Publishing Company.

Gillis, H. L. & Bonney, W. C. (1986). Group counseling with couples or families: Adding adventure activities. *Journal for Specialists in Group Work. 11*(4), 213–219.

Rohnke, K. (1989). *Cowstails and cobras II.* Hamilton, MA: Project Adventure, Inc. 103–104.

Schoel, J., Prouty, D., & Radcliff, P. (1988). *Islands of healing: A guide to adventure-based counseling.* Hamilton, MA: Project

Tobler, N. S. (1986). Meta-analysis of 143 drug prevention programs: Quantitative outcome results of program participants compared to a control or comparison group. *Journal of Drug Issues. 16*, 537–568.

THE ETHICS OF FACILITATION: DOING THE RIGHT THINGS WITH THE RIGHT PEOPLE

Thinking without learning is useless;
learning without thinking is dangerous.

While it is not the intent of this book to offer a full discourse on the ethics of facilitating adventure experiences (readers are referred to other sources such as Hunt, 1990; Mitten, 1994; and Gass & Wurdinger, 1993), it is important to consider appropriate professional conduct when providing client facilitation. While all professionals are ultimately responsible for themselves, their actions, and their duty to their clients, dependence on this type of "individualistic approach" to being responsible is often destined to fail in the larger "system" of developing and furthering the aims of a field. Often the actions of one or a few professionals can misrepresent and undermine the appropriate and positive efforts of others (for an example in adventure programming, see Matthews, 1993).

How does a profession combine individual duty within the broader system of professional conduct? One approach has been to advance principles, standards, or guidelines of ethical behavior. Ethics addresses what is *right or correct* behavior. And while it is possible to be unprofessional and still not unethical (e.g., showing up late for client appointments might be unprofessional, but probably wouldn't be unethical) (Corey, Corey, & Callahan, 1993), concern for ethical behavior serves as one of the key cornerstones for any professional decision. Designing the proper facilitation of client experiences can be an ethical decision and may need to be considered by the facilitator.

As many of the techniques in the exercises outlined in this book indicate, when the sophistication of facilitating and working with clients increases so does the need to look at the appropriateness of how experiences are conducted. As one can see, framing experiences asks

19

clients to consider concentrating on one set of outcomes and processes, quite often at the expense of other focuses. While this may increase the effectiveness of the intervention, it also runs the risk of enhancing the misappropriateness of the experience. Can one avoid this problem by choosing not to facilitate? Probably not, since avoiding any facilitation of an experience doesn't free a facilitator from ethical scrutiny; such a conclusion itself can be an ethical decision.

If professionals find themselves in this dilemma, what guidelines should they follow? Some guidelines professionals may wish to consider include:

1. It seems that experiences, and their appropriate facilitation, work best when the focus of the facilitator's efforts is done with *empathy for the client*. When facilitators are motivated to use processing techniques to "look good," wield power over clients, or reach their own personal gains, questions of appropriateness and lasting effectiveness for the client seem to come into question. To achieve the appropriate focus on empathy, several principles can be valuable to follow. Some of these may include:

   a. Above all else, do no harm to the client.
   b. Make sure that facilitation efforts are done with the client's best interests in mind.
   c. The focus of the interventions is to serve the client, not the facilitator.
   d. There is purpose in the reason for using the particular technique.
   e. It "feels right" to the professional.
   f. It is something the professional would be willing to stand up in front of other colleagues and say that they used this technique and state why.
   g. Only use those techniques that you would want to be used with you if you were the client (i.e., the "golden rule").
   h. Remind yourself that the experience possesses the resources to be more influential than the facilitator's best efforts in helping the client.
   i. When in doubt, follow rule #1.

2. Kitchener (1984) identified five basic moral principles as being the most critical for professionals in the "helping professions" to follow. These five include:

a. *Autonomy*—Individuals have the right to freedom of action and choice as long as their behavior does not infringe upon the rights of others.
b. *Nonmaleficence*—Above all, no harm will be done.
c. *Beneficence*—The focus of a professional's actions is to contribute to the health and welfare of others.
d. *Fidelity*—Be faithful, keep promises, be loyal and respectful of a person's rights.
e. *Justice*—Individuals will be treated as equals, which implies the concept of "fairness."

3. From a systemic perspective on the implementation of ethical principles for facilitating, work by the AEE's Therapeutic Adventure Professional Group (TAPG) (with assistance from the American Psychological Association and the American Association for Marriage and Family Therapy) and the *Manual of Accreditation Standards for Adventure Programs* (Williamson & Gass, 1993) has advanced the following guidelines for professionals that merit investigation:

1. *Staff conduct experiences with an appropriate level of competence.*

Explanation: Professionals promote and conduct activities within the level of their competence. This includes, but may not be limited to: (a) providing services within the boundaries of their competence based on education, training, supervision, experience, and practice; (b) taking reasonable steps to ensure the competence of their work; (c) avoiding situations where personal problems or conflicts will impair their work performance or judgment; (d) staying abreast of current information in the field; and (e) participating in ongoing professional efforts to maintain their knowledge, practice, and skills.

2. *Staff conduct experiences with integrity.*

Explanation: Professionals conduct activities with honesty, fairness, and respect, in interactions with both participants and peers. This includes, but may not be limited to: (a) no false, misleading, or deceptive statements are made when describing or reporting qualifications, services, products, or fees; and (b) being aware of how their own belief systems, values, needs, and limitations affect participants.

3. *Staff conduct experiences in a responsible manner.*

Explanation: Professionals uphold the ethical principles of their work. This includes, but may not be limited to: (a) being clear with participants as to their roles and obligations as a professional; (b) accepting responsibility for their behavior and decisions; (c) adapting methods to the needs of different populations; (d) possessing an adequate basis for professional judgments; (e) not beginning services when the constraints of limited contact will not benefit participant needs; (f) continuing services only so long as it is reasonably clear that participants will benefit from services; and (g) conducting experiences in a manner that results in minimal impact and no permanent damage to the environment.

4. *Staff conduct experiences with respect for the rights and dignity of participants.*

Explanation: Professionals respect the fundamental rights, dignity, and worth of all people. They respect participants' rights to privacy, confidentiality, and self-determination within the limits of the law and the mission statement of the Association for Experiential Education. Professionals also strive to be sensitive to cultural and individual differences—including those due to age, gender, race, ethnicity, national origin, religion, sexual orientation, disability, and socioeconomic status. Professionals do not engage in sexual or other harassment or exploitation of participants. Other concerns include, but may not be limited to: (a) respecting participants' rights to make decisions and helping them understand the consequences of their choices; and (b) providing participants with appropriate information about the nature of services and their rights, risks, and responsibilities. They also provide an opportunity to discuss the results, interpretations, and conclusions with participants, (a) respecting participants' rights to refuse consent to services and activities; (b) obtaining informed consent from participants and, when appropriate, parents or guardians before beginning services; and (c) accurately representing their competence, training, education, and experience relevant to the program being delivered.

5. *Staff are concerned for the well-being of participants.*

Explanation: Professionals are sensitive to participant needs and well-being. Professionals provide for the appropriate physical needs of participants, including necessary water, nutrition, clothing, shelter, rest, or other essentials and monitor the appropriate use of emotional and physical risk in adventure experiences.

Other areas of consideration include, but may not be limited to: (a) assisting in obtaining other services if the program cannot, for appropriate reasons, provide the professional help participants may need; (b) planning experiences with the intent that decisions made during and after are in accordance with the participants' best interests; (c) respecting participants' rights to decide the extent to which confidential material can be made public, except under extreme conditions (e.g., when required by law to prevent a clear and immediate danger to a person or persons, if permission has previously been obtained in writing).

   6. *Staff recognize their level of social responsibility.*

Explanation: Professionals are aware of their responsibilities to community and society. Areas include, but are not limited to: (a) appropriately encouraging the development of standards and policies that serve their participants' interests as well as those of the public; and (b) respecting the property of others.

   7. *Staff avoid dual relationships with participants that impair professional judgment.*

Explanation: Professionals avoid exploiting or misleading participants, as well as others, during or after professional relationships. This is accomplished by intentionally avoiding dual relationships with participants that impair professional judgement. This includes but is not limited to: (a) business or close personal relationships; (b) sexual relationships; or (c) inappropriate physical contact.

REFERENCES

Corey, G., Corey, M. S., & Callahan, P. (1993). *Issues and ethics in the helping professions*. Pacific Grove, CA: Brooks/Cole Publishing Company.

Gass, M. A. & Wurdinger, S. (1993). Ethical decisions in experience-based training and development programs. *Journal of Experiential Education, 16*(2), 41–47.

Hunt, J. (1990). *Ethical issues in experiential education*. Boulder, CO: Association for Experiential Education.

Kitchener, K. S. (1984). Intuition, critical evaluation, and ethical principles: The foundation for ethical decisions in counseling psychology. *The Counseling Psychologist, 12*(3), 43–55.

Matthews, M. (1993). Wilderness programs offer promising alternatives for some youth; more regulation likely. In M. A. Gass (Ed.), *Adventure therapy: Therapeutic applications of adventure programming,* (pp. 239–252). Boulder, CO: Association for Experiential Education.

Mitten, D. (1994). Ethical considerations in adventure therapy: A feminist critique. In E. Cole, E. Erdman, & E. Rothblom (Eds.), *Wilderness therapy for women: The power of adventure.* Binghamton, NY: Harrington Park Press.

Williamson, J. & Gass, M. A. (1993). *Manual of accreditation standards for adventure programs.* Boulder, CO: Association for Experiential Education.

THERAPEUTIC POPULATIONS

PARENTS' QUALITY CALL

INTRODUCTION

This activity can be used with a variety of groups, but in this particular case it was used with adults during a three-hour "couples only" session of a five-day family enrichment program (i.e., "enrichment" as compared with recreational, adjunctive, or primary therapy adventure programs). It was designed as the second activity of this session, which was during the evening of the first night of the program. The initiative does not require extreme risk-taking, except in terms of being unable to see because your eyes are closed, and physical touch (which may be difficult for some participants). This is a good assessment activity for a number of things, some of which may include: (1) determining group members' ability to follow directions and take risks; (2) gathering an idea of the roles these individuals play in group settings; (3) observing each individual's comfort with conflict and frustration; (4) beginning to get an idea of each individual's degree of comfort in working with other parents as resources of information; and (5) examining how spouses work independently of one another.

GOALS

The initiative, presented in this manner, emphasizes: (1) what group members perceive as healthy attributes to be working on as parents in families; (2) the similarity of what parents are looking for to make their families better than what they already are; (3) "normalizing" the interaction of parents asking for help from other parents in the group; (4) emphasizing that all families can use more of "something" to help be more functional; (5) increasing the level of sharing of ideas among couples; and (6) having fun and setting a tone for fun during activities in this session as well as during the week.

SET-UP

The set-up for this initiative is much like the Hog Call initiative (see *Silver Bullets* by Rohnke, 1984, pp. 98–99). Parents of the group are asked to "pair up" with someone they don't know well yet, but who looks like a person they might seek out for advice on parenting (not their spouse!). If there is an odd number of people (e.g., single parents taking part in the program), one group can form a trio. After this is accomplished, have each pair or trio take five minutes to introduce themselves to each other, as well as decide on the qualities that they are seeking assistance with and share that quality with their partner(s). This quality doesn't have to be something that is difficult for them, but may be a thing that if they had more assistance with or just more of, would make them feel more capable as a parent. In sharing this quality with their partner(s), each person should take approximately 30 seconds to describe what this means so their partner(s) understand it. They should not share this quality with other pairs at this time, but should be reminded to remember their quality as well as their partner's quality.

After this is accomplished, the pair decides who will be "it." Have all of the "its" join hands with one facilitator and close their eyes, and the "not its" do the same with the other facilitator. (Note: Being "it" or "not it" really makes no difference in this game. A number of other methods can be used to divide up pairs. I use this because it provides me with some insight into how people will react to "self-choosing" behaviors given a traditional paradigm.)

Participants are told to keep their eyes closed while they are randomly distributed in the "playing area" and not to move until they are directed to do so. The playing area should be large enough to move around in, but small enough for people to hear each other and the facilitator. If participants are not aware of the "bumper's up" position, they should be taught this at the beginning of the activity.

SAMPLE PRESENTATION

(Participants are asked to stand in a circle.) "We'd like to do an activity that people may find enjoyable and sometimes eye-opening. One of the things I am aware of as a parent is that there are a lot of times that can be particularly troublesome or trying. It could be putting kids to sleep at night, potty training, juggling 15 things at once, having your child going out on their first date . . . do you know what I mean? Can anyone else share a time like this?" (I look to others to share brief statements representing their projection of parental interactions that they see as difficult—others include temper tantrums, getting kids to study, curfews, etc. Sharing a brief humorous anecdote often sets a light tone for this type of sharing.)

"One of the things I know in dealing with these times is that there are certain qualities that may be extremely important for me in my role as a parent. It seems when I have these qualities, it makes these times go so much easier and I feel more capable as a parent. What we want for you to do is to think in your mind of one of these qualities, and when you have chosen one that can be represented by a single word, raise you right hand. This quality doesn't have to be something that is difficult for you, but maybe something that if you had more assistance with or just more of, would make parenting much easier. Don't share your word out loud right now with others—we will be doing this later."

(After everyone has their hand up.) "Okay, what I would like you to do right now is look around the group and, if you haven't already, notice the tremendous wealth of parental resources we have here." (Pause for a few seconds and have them look around.) "What we want you to do is to 'pair up' with someone you don't know well yet, but who looks like a person you might seek out for advice on parenting (not your spouse!)."

(After this is accomplished.) "What we'd like you to do now in your pairs or trio is to take five minutes to introduce yourselves, share a bit about yourself, and tell the quality you thought of earlier that you find so important. When sharing the single word that represents this quality, make sure you take no more than 30 seconds to describe what this word means so your partner understands it. Do not share this quality with other pairs at this time, but make sure that you remember your partner's quality as well as yours. Your partner will be serving as an important resource for you in this activity, as well as others, and it is critical that you remember these qualities that both of you have spoken about."

(After this has been accomplished.) "Now what we would like you to do is in your pair decide who is 'it' and who is 'not it.' I'd like the 'its' to come over with me and the 'not its' to go over with Mike. Before you go, make sure that you remember your partner's word as well as yours." (After they get to the intended spot.) "What we want you to do is join hands, close your eyes, and let us place you around in different spots in the field, okay? Don't move or speak until we tell you."

(After everyone is set.) "Now what we want you to do to try to find your partner using the following rules: (1) The only word you may speak is the quality that you are in search of. For example, if the quality I shared was 'patience,' this is the only word I can speak in searching for my partner. I know it might be tempting, but you can't say: 'Hey, Bill, I'm over here,' or even use their word for their quality. The only word you may use in the process of finding your partner is the quality that you're in search of; (2) you may not open your eyes, as tempting as it might be, until you find your partner or you feel unsafe and need to open them; (3) when you find your partner, open your eyes, do a brief sort of congratulations, but then remain silent until everyone else has completed their search. If you understand these three rules, we would like you to get into the 'bumper position' we showed your earlier. If you have any questions, raise one hand and I will call on you. Is everyone ready? Okay, begin."

LOGISTICS

All proper safety issues should be followed (e.g., making sure there are no obstacles that people will run into or trip on, reinforcing that people have their hands up in a "bumper" position and move at a safe speed while they are walking with their eyes closed). As a beginning activity, I would recommend not "blindfolding" individuals, choosing instead the "challenge by choice" option of keeping their eyes closed themselves. As an initial activity, I don't feel I know them well enough to know if having a blindfold on is appropriate for them or not. As a facilitator, I remain out of the activity to facilitate any potential safety issues as well as observe how the participants solve their dilemma of searching for their partner(s). As people finish the activity, I encourage them to remain silent until the activity is completed by everyone.

Note that, in conducting the activity, if shouting during the activity contraindicates the objective of the experience, whispering can be used in its place.

DEBRIEFING

I usually begin by having the parents sit down and introduce their partner to the group, stating the word their partner used and why they used it. "Checking in" is reinforced between partners to make sure people feel that they are represented accurately. This process usually reaches most of the objectives set for the activity that are listed earlier. Other things to do might include:

1. Presenting the term "BFOs" (i.e., Blinding Flashes of the Obvious) to label and encourage insights participants may have about the activity. For example, it's quite common that a lot of parents choose the same words (e.g., patience and communica-

tion), which can present an interesting BFO or "aha" experience. I have found that it is extremely enriching for the group to see the similarity of the needs they have as parents.
2. Possibly discussing how areas of conflict or frustration were handled. Are these processes which we want to use in the future?
3. The dynamic of the final people completing the activity can be very interesting with some groups.

Questions posed may include:

■ If people were "stuck" in looking for a particular answer, what was our role as a group in helping them?
■ Should we as a group help them or let them figure it out for themselves?
■ It seems almost obvious that in the process being "laughed with" is much preferable to being "laughed at," but how do we want to handle these challenges when they arise for this group in the next activities?

CONTRIBUTORS

Michael A. Gass, PhD
University of New Hampshire
New Hampshire Hall
124 Main Street
Durham, NH 03824-3559, USA
(603) 862-2024

Anna Kay Vorsteg, Program Director
Merrowvista Education Center
Canaan Road
Ossipee, NH 03864, USA
(603) 539-6607

FAMILY STRENGTHS PROTECTOR

INTRODUCTION

This initiative is designed for use with families participating in an adventure therapy program. It works most effectively in programs using a multi-family group format. This activity asks families to engage in self-disclosure. Because of this, the best time to introduce the activity is after the families have had an opportunity to get to know the other families and the program format.

GOALS

The initiative emphasizes: (1) the family's strengths, (2) some means to "protect" the family's strengths, and (3) the effects of stress on the family system.

MATERIALS

Each family group is given crayons, a raw egg, 25 straws, and about 35 inches of masking tape.

SAMPLE PRESENTATION

(After the materials are distributed to each family.) "This initiative is called the Family Strengths Protector. First, we want you to discuss all those strengths and characteristics of your family you would not want to lose. Make sure each family member has an opportunity to state his or her opinion. These strengths are to be written on the egg with the crayons.

Next, discuss all those behaviors, skills, and coping mechanisms that can be used by your family members to protect the family's strengths. The straws and tape represent these protective mechanisms. Your task is to create, as a family unit, a Family Strengths Protector using the straws and tape. These are the only materials you can use to protect your family strengths/egg. The purpose of the Strengths Protector Mechanism is to prevent the cracking or breaking of the family's strengths/egg when exposed to stress and sudden shock. The egg and its 'carrier' will be dropped onto the floor from a ladder."

The families should be given about 20–30 minutes to complete their designs. The facilitator ensures that each family has enough time to create their egg protector unit and then asks all of the families to gather around the ladder.

Presenter: "The ladder represents external stressors in a family's life. These are stressors that can weaken or crack your family's strengths. You and your family will present your Family Strengths Protector to the rest of the group by: (1) describing your family's strengths, (2) discussing those behaviors and mechanisms that you will use to protect your family's strengths, and (3) deciding, as a family, how far up the ladder you will go to drop your Family Strengths Protector with the knowledge that the higher up you go, the more stress you will place on the family's strengths/egg. You will be allowed to drop the egg as many times as you choose as long as the egg stays intact. In other words, you have the option to start off testing the effects of stress on your family's strengths/egg by dropping it off the lower ladder rungs and then working your way up to the higher rungs. This method will allow you to subject your strengths/egg more gradually to higher levels of stress."

The facilitator gives each family an opportunity to present their Family Strengths Protector. The facilitator can be the person who drops the egg, but must first ask the family how and from what rung they want it dropped. The facilitator can also spot one of the family members as that person drops the egg from the ladder.

DEBRIEFING

Most of the debriefing occurs as the families discuss their strengths, their protective mechanisms, and the effects of stress on their family. Some questions that can be used during the activity include:

1. Who (which family member) stated what strengths?
2. What do you, as other families, think are the strengths of this family?
3. What are some of the skills you, as a family, believe will protect your strengths?
4. What are some additional skills and behaviors that you will need to use in the future to protect your family's strengths?
5. What types of stress are common for your family at this point in time?
6. What types of stress are anticipated in the future?

CONTRIBUTOR

Jackie Gerstein, EdD, NCC
2 Raudo Place
Sante Fe, NM 87505, USA
(505) 466-7758

PLEASE BE SEATED

INTRODUCTION

This initiative has specific applications for couples and other dyads who are working toward a mutually supportive relationship. It can also be used in groups to help individuals become more aware of their own style and needs with regard to giving and receiving guidance. This is a good assessment activity to determine unique styles of offering and accepting support. It also provides a wealth of information for current or later discussions.

GOALS

This initiative emphasizes: (1) the intricacy of giving guidance to a partner, (2) the intricacy of accepting guidance from a partner, (3) the aspects of healthy constructive guidance versus critical, negative guidance, and (4) how the individual being guided would like to receive information.

SET-UP

The set-up for this initiative is fairly simple. The couple(s) are asked to think of a situation where they would (or have) looked to their partner for support and guidance. They then share this briefly with one another and the group, depending on group size and time constraints. This situation becomes the "path" they will walk and a chair represents the end goal they wish to reach. The partners then take turns being blindfolded and following the instructions of their sighted partner as they attempt to reach their designated chair and sit down. The blindfolded participant may not reach out to be certain the chair is there before she or he sits down. Safety precautions include providing an area with enough obstacles to make it interesting without it being an area where one false step could be dangerous. If several pairs are working at a time, the sighted participants must work together to avoid collisions.

SAMPLE PRESENTATION

Participants are asked to pair up with partners. "People working together in partnerships often take turns giving and receiving guidance from one another. What are some things you appreciate about receiving guidance? What are some things you don't appreciate?" A discussion of the different reactions to guidance is facilitated. "Offering guidance can also be pretty tricky. What do you enjoy about giving your partner guidance? What do you find difficult about giving guidance?" A discussion about the different reactions to giving guidance is facilitated. "Now, take five minutes with your partner. Use the first two minutes to come up with a situation in your life where you would like your partner to provide you with guidance. It can be anything from learning a new skill, such as changing a tire, to receiving feedback on how to improve your relationships with your parents. You will be taking turns being blindfolded. The partner with sight will verbally guide the partner who is blind through a path to a chair. The path represents the process of working through your chosen situation. The chair represents the end goal, such as a new tire on the car or an improved relationship with your parents. The guiding partner may not offer any assistance other than verbal information. No touching or moving obstacles is allowed. Now, take a few minutes to decide on a situation and to share that with your partner." (Allow an allotted time for this interaction.) "Now, choose who will be blindfolded first. Once you have walked through the exercise, switch roles and do it again. Throughout the experience, pay attention to what you are feeling and reacting to. If it feels like it would be helpful, offer your partner some feedback, but resist getting too bogged down to the point that you don't continue the exercise." The couples are then given a chance to try the initiative.

LOGISTICS

I choose to remain as an observer in this activity. This allows me to observe the interactions and either offer feedback at the time or during debriefing. It may be helpful with a large group to split them in two and let half observe while the other half experience the exercise, and then switch.

DEBRIEFING

Initially, a process of sharing between the partners is useful to briefly discuss what happened and how it felt to be in the different roles. With a large group, two pairs can be encouraged to debrief together. Finally, a large group discussion should be facilitated. Questions such as: "What was it like to receive guidance? What was it like to be responsible to offer guidance? How could the guidance have been more helpful? What did you do to improve your giving or receiving during the activity? What could you have done? What was it like to finally sit in the chair?"

When this initiative is done with a couple in a more therapeutic context, more specific framing can be utilized. The couple can also be encouraged to process further and to redo the exercise trying out new approaches based on what developed from the initial experience.

CONTRIBUTOR

Betsy Hearn
Macalester College
Office of Community Service
1600 Grand Avenue
St. Paul, MN 55105, USA
(612) 696–6040

THE POWER STRUGGLE
(THE RELATIONSHIP DANCE)

INTRODUCTION/LOGISTICS

Name of Activity: Stand Off

Number of Participants: Activity is done in pairs; total group size can vary greatly.

Target Population(s): Couples primarily; could also be used with parent/child pairs, friends, co-workers, supervisor/employee pairs, and others.

Treatment Issues: Power struggles; similarities/differences in relating styles; cooperation and trust within relationships; aggression and violence versus passivity and dependence.

Description of Activity: Couples/pairs stand face-to-face, feet together with their toes approximately 12 inches apart. Couples raise hands to shoulder height and place palms of hands flat against partner's palms. The goal of the activity is to off-balance the other by pushing against his/her palms so that he/she has to move one or both feet to maintain balance.

Dynamics of the Activity: Each partner will deal with the built-in (however slight) aggressiveness of the activity in a way that is indicative of his/her interaction style. Competitiveness, assertiveness, aggressiveness, and power will likely look and feel different than passivity, accommodation, co-dependence, and weakness/powerlessness. The style of each partner should be apparent, especially after they experience a few rounds and begin to talk about their inner experience and their perceptions of the other person.

GOALS

The intent is that the interactions will highlight how each person approaches their relationship. The assumption is that behavior with one's partner is consistent over time. Becoming more aware of this behavior and exploring whether the interactive behaviors represent patterns played out between the partners are the primary purposes of the activity. There may be important insights from unexamined or unconscious ways of relating. If the partners can openly discuss how their interactions are similar or different from their daily interactions, there will likely be important issues to explore and benefit from. They also may find that their styles in this activity are not typical and this may point to other issues worth exploring (e.g., neglected aspects of one or both partners' needs, desires, strengths, feelings).

DEBRIEFING

As stated above, the intent is to have couples identify their styles (or strategies) for off-balancing their partner and to explore whether these styles represent typical patterns of interacting at home. There are numerous couple styles: aggressive/passive, assertive/assertive, accommodating/accommodating, dominating/dependent, weak/strong, strong/strong, etc. Sharing between each couple should identify patterns and lead to further discussion. Open sharing among the couples should emphasize differences and a diversity of ways of relating that should be interesting and provocative.

Themes for Processing: Some couples may experience a struggle for power or control, and competition ("Is this similar to what happens at home?"). Others may find themselves in a one-sided exchange ("What does each gain and lose in this way of relating?"). Others may find themselves in more of a "dance" than in a struggle ("Is this indicative of how they relate as a couple? Is this the result of some evolution/change in their relationship over time?").

Some couples may notice that often there is no "winner," because if one partner falls off balance the other often does too. They may have ended up "playing" with the give-and-take of the interaction.

Did the couples maintain or avoid eye contact during the activity? What significance does this hold for them?

What do couples often struggle over/about: money, parenting, roles, sex, power, equity, family responsibilities? Do the styles of interacting experienced in this activity find their way into these struggles? How do these ways of struggling/interacting affect the successful resolution of the struggle?

The theme of "projective-identifications" or "unconscious collusions" may be appropriate depending on the background of the therapist and the goal of the clients.

Variations: Sequence: First do a "stand off" in the same manner but with the striking of palms (more forceful interaction); then do the activity as described above, but in slow motion. This progression may lead to the idea that cooperation and "a dance" is more productive and suggestive of a style the couple may want to explore. Adding a "squat thrust" may bring up other responses. This activity is the same, except that the partners squat down on the balls of their feet with their knees almost touching. Finally, one or both partners could be blindfolded to increase the vulnerability quotient and to add to the discussion.

Sculpting: Other individuals could be added (physically or mentally) to the interaction. "Where do your children fit in this power struggle? Whose side are they on? Whom do they root for? Do either of you enlist their support? Do you actively try to hide your struggles from them? What triangles are suggested by your answers to these questions? What are the implications?" A child or children could actually join the struggle by helping one of the partners or by trying to keep each partner from actually winning or by trying to stop the interaction.

If the partners are friends, co-workers, or supervisor/employee, then appropriate questions could be framed to fit the typical interaction setting. Others could be added to the struggle to play out their typical role(s) in the interaction.

CONTRIBUTORS

Jo Ann Orr
The Family Expedition Program
New Hampshire Hall
124 Main Street
Durham, NH 03824-3559, USA
(603) 862-2070

Jim Moore
Recreation Program
6 Old Carver
Western Washington University
Bellingham, WA 98225-9067, USA
(206) 650-3540

UTILIZATION THEORY:
FAMILY ROLES AND THE BLIND SQUARE

INTRODUCTION

This introduction is designed for an individual family or with a group addressing family roles. The activity should be utilized well after the issue of family roles has been addressed. The therapist should have a high degree of comfort with the roles taken on by individuals in the group/family. The power of this introduction comes in using actual elements of a person's role and prescribing this behavior. For this description, I utilize the classic family roles found in addiction counseling. This includes the "Hero," the "Scapegoat," the "Mascot," the "Lost Child," the "Chief Enabler," and the "Alcoholic." The initiative I use is the Blind Square; however this introduction could be utilized with other activities as well.

GOALS

The goals of this activity are to: (1) heighten the awareness of an individual's role in the family, (2) raise discussion about family roles; and (3) provide a concrete experience of an individual's role in his/her family.

SET-UP

This activity begins with each member of the family/group wearing a blindfold. A portion of a rope is then laid in each person's hands.

SAMPLE PRESENTATION

"We have been talking about family roles and the role you take in your family. I am going to provide you with an opportunity to take on this role. This activity is about how you complete tasks in your family. It is called the Blind Square. When we begin, your task as a family will be to create a perfect square using all the rope. Before beginning, I want to help you remember the roles you have identified for yourself and help you embrace this role.

Let's start with Dad. George, you talked about things needing to be done your way, and that it is really hard for you to change. That no matter how much you yell and scream, nothing gets done . . . and that is why you drink. So for this activity, these issues are your rules. You must shout and scream everything you say, but you cannot move or be moved along the rope, nor may you let go of the rope. Doris, you have talked about really wanting things to change, but being scared of this as well; also about really doubting George's sincerity about quitting drinking. Your rules for this activity are that you must also yell and shout everything you say; however you can only say things that directly conflict or agree with what George says. You can be moved by others but you can't move yourself or others, and you must stay on the rope at all times. Bobby, you have been so quiet, so we'd like you to follow that strength in your role. Your rules will be to not say anything and to go wherever you like, letting the rope go if you wish. Jane, you have talked about this being a joke, about getting in trouble a lot because of what is happening at home. You said that if people would just lighten up things would get better. Your rules for this activity will be two things: to lighten things up, but also to express the anger in the same way you have done so far. So, in order to do this, you must shout everything you say, but you may only use foul language. You also may leave the rope at any time. Sue, you have said you wished your brother and sister were more reasonable, that if they just took things more seriously and helped out more around the house the fighting would stop. You have a few rules. You can talk, but not shout. You must stay on the rope. You can move along the rope, but you cannot jump over people. As in your family, you are responsible for assessing whether the group has successfully completed the task.

Let me repeat the rules:

George—You must shout and scream everything you say, but you cannot move or be moved along the rope, nor may you let go of the rope.

Doris—You must also yell and shout everything you say; however you can only say things that directly conflict or agree with what George says.

Bobby—You cannot say anything, but you can go wherever you like, letting the rope go if you wish.

Jane—You must shout everything you say, but you may only use foul language. You may leave the rope at any time.

Sue—You can talk, but not shout. You must stay on the rope. You can move along the rope, but you cannot jump over people. You are responsible for assessing whether the group has successfully completed its task.

Let me repeat—this activity is about how you as a family complete tasks, how you negotiate to get things done, and what you are willing to do to complete your family's tasks. You will have 45 minutes to complete this activity. If there are no questions you may begin."

DEBRIEFING

Expect a lot of frustration, confusion, and resentment at this activity. Allow for plenty of time to vent these feeling. Possible debriefing/processing questions or topics include: "How comfortable were the rules for you?" "How well did they fit you?" "What did your role contribute to the success/failure of this activity, what does it contribute to your family?" "What did you like about your role?" "What would you like to change about your role and the rules you play by?"

ADDITIONAL SET-UP THOUGHTS

Several additional options exist for the set-up of this activity. They include: (1) Have family members take on another person's role (you can switch to this midstream or set it up at first this way), (2) allow them to change the rules the way they want to (perhaps midstream), (3) change someone's rules without telling the rest of the group (e.g., make the alcoholic mute and able to see, symbolizing her/his newness to the program, her/his desire to change, but difficulty utilizing this information), and (4) have them repeat the activity with different rules/roles (this would be most useful as they actually change their roles in the family).

CONTRIBUTOR

Christian Itin, MSW
1350 Balsam Avenue
Boulder, CO 80304, USA
(303) 442-2189

THE TRUST TRIANGLE:
A METAPHOR FOR RELATIONSHIPS

INTRODUCTION

This trust initiative is a variation on the traditional low ropes element often called the Wild Woosey or Low V. I first encountered this version at the Pretty Lake Adventure Centre in Kalamazoo, MI, several years ago. Since then, the more I've used this event, the more I've grown in appreciation of its metaphoric richness and its value as a tool for understanding and working with relationships.

GOALS

When framed as follows, the Trust Triangle emphasizes an individual's style of being in a relationship with others. The initiative provides an opportunity to explore the behavorial qualities that are manifested in healthy relationships, as well as to experience the pitfalls of less effective aspects of behavioral interaction. This framing is especially valuable for working with couples, parent-teens, or co-workers who are in a close working relationship.

SET-UP

The physical set-up for the Trust Triangle differs from Wild Woosey ropes events in that as the wires diverge they reach a point where they again begin to come back together. It also differs by including an "obstacle tree" midway between the beginning point and wide-point. The advantage of this arrangement is that the event now has a beginning, middle, and end, as well as obstacles along the way. This design lends to the framing and also can give a sense of accomplishment to the total activity.

The task, as with other versions of this event, is for a pair of individuals to move along the cables supporting each other, eventually using the method of keeping hands high and body straight and leaning together. Additionally, it is necessary for participants to alternate hands to get around the obstacle tree without touching it. Also, as they reach the wide-point, one participant, while still leaning on their partner, must step around the inside of the wide-point tree, and then both continue until they reach the final tree.

The safety considerations are the same as for other versions (e.g., no interlocking fingers, walkers should step off wire if fall is eminent). Spotting initially begins with all spotters outside the cables, and, as soon as possible, begin to add spotters inside the cables until there are only two spotters outside the cables for each participant. It also seems to add to the process if inside spotters are in a standing position, facing each other, with arms out (zippered as if they were doing a trust fall) and positioned directly under the torso of the person they are spotting. This position seems to allow much more interaction between spotters and participants than the "bending over spotting method."

SAMPLE PRESENTATION

"These cables can be viewed as a model for two people in a relationship. Each partner walks their own path (the cables), but they each choose to stay together and share their journey, supporting each other along the way. For just a moment, imagine two people who might be in some type of relationship out in the world. They could be spouses, friends, or co-workers. What are some ways these two people might support each other in a relationship?" Typical responses here include: listening to each other, trusting that you can count on the other to be there, giving whatever help is asked, etc.

"In this event you'll have an opportunity to provide support in ways that you just mentioned. In addition, you'll get a chance to demonstrate support for your partner physically." At this point, state the task, demonstrate traverse technique, safety considerations, and spotting. Allow one pair of participants to proceed with the traverse.

"After watching these two on the wires, what parallels do you see between this activity and relationships?" As in other versions of this event, typical initial responses include: in relationships you have to lean on each other; you have to communicate; eye contact is important; you have to trust that the other person will be there for you; it takes commitment; you must move together; one can't get too far ahead; etc.

"As you give this a try and as you watch others do it, see if you notice additional ways that this activity can represent relationships." Another pair attempts the traverse. Throughout the event, the facilitator may also want to jot down actual dialogue from the participants as they traverse, to be read back later during debrief. Much of what is said while on the wires has direct parallels to the language of relationships (e.g., it's OK to lean on me, tell me what you need). Participants continue to go in pairs with brief processing after each traverse. If a pair falls along the way, process what happened and have them return to the last tree successfully negotiated and begin again.

At the beginning: At first, you don't really know each other, things are very shaky, and you're not sure if you can even make it with this person. You can be so close or intertwined with your partner (dependent) that it makes it difficult to maintain your own balance.

In the middle: When we each have our own space (independence), we are better able to lend true support. No matter how strong I am, I can't do it for you. Regardless of my strength, when the distance gets really wide (difficulties great), I must have your help if we're going to make it together (interdependence). When I encounter obstacles (problems), I must remember that the obstacle isn't going anywhere and that the way I get through it is by not losing focus on where my support is coming from (my partner). When difficulties arise, it's important to: (1) identify what I need, (2) verbalize it, (3) make sure I get it or try again. Even though my partner may say what they need, I may not give it, thinking I know better what they need. This often occurs with a large person refusing to give weight to a smaller person, for fear of pushing them off, and as a result the smaller person falls forward due to lack of support (i.e., by "protecting" their partner from their "burdensome weight" they have inadvertently created a downfall). It's all practice. If we fall, we learn something and we can try again, backing up to where it was working for us. If we are really going to make it together, we have to find a balance point where each of us is getting our needs met.

At the end: Even though we communicated well back there, things keep changing, so we can't stop talking to each other. When we encounter the same old problems again (wires close), it helps to remember how we got through them before. It feels good to make it through the hard stuff and come out the other side.

DEBRIEFING

Debriefing questions that may be posed include: "To you, how does the arrangement of the cables themselves represent a relationship? (e.g., sometimes close, sometimes distant; keeps changing; each has own path with different problems; it's possible to do it, but usually not easy). In a relationship, what might the obstacles represent? (e.g., variety of life problems). Who would the spotters represent? (e.g., friends, family, support group, counselors, any outside perspective). When you were getting advice from your spotters, how much did you listen? How much did you use their advice? How aware of your spotters were you when you were on the wire? How would it have been different if they weren't there? In life, who exactly are your spotters? In life, who would most like to see you succeed? If you learn by watching others model successful strategies to make it through here, who are your models for successful relationships 'out there'?"

After discussing these points as a group, have partners break away in pairs (or individually with journals) to reflect on: "How much was my behavior on the wire like my behavior in relationships? What did I do here that was effective? What strategies do I need to use more? How much was I able to modify my own behavior and adopt successful strategies when I ran into difficulties on the line? What insights did I have about myself or about relationships in general? How can I use this information in my life relationships?" (If with spouse or significant other, "What commitment can I make to my partner based on what I learned about myself in relationships?")

FINAL NOTE

A true test as to the relevance of any metaphoric process in the "real world" is: "How much does it get used? Does it actually make a difference in one's life?"

Well, in my relationship with my partner Debbie, I can safely say that the Trust Triangle has been our most "used" experiential reference point from the ropes course. We have often found ourselves in the midst of a problem, perhaps stuck and not seeing a way through, when one or the other of us says something like: "Hey, I'm really stretched out here. I'm falling and I need you to listen. And by the way, look me in the eyes." This usually allows us to shift gears enough to give each other a knowing smile. At this point we are each back on the wire, remembering what it is we've learned there, remembering how we each have our own way, and also remembering that we've chosen to do it together.

CONTRIBUTOR

Anthony Curtis
Adventureworks, Inc.
1300 Narrows of the Harpeth
Kingston Springs, TN 37082, USA
(615) 952-4720

RECOVERY CHALLENGES

INTRODUCTION

The following is a series of activities and metaphoric introductions designed to address each of the 12 steps of the Alcoholics Anonymous process. Within each Logistics section are inferential elaborations and reconstructions of client issues that can be made throughout the experience. Following each Debriefing section is additional information and possible paradoxes that exist in each experience.

STEP ONE

"We admit we are powerless over our addiction and that our lives have become unmanageable."

The focus of this process is on the illusion of control and paradox of dependence on abusive substances for power.

SET-UP

Life Walk. This consists of a length of cable or rope, no more than 2 feet off the ground, stretched between two stable points, about 10 feet apart (Mohawk Traverse, Rohnke, 1989).

SAMPLE PRESENTATION

"This cable is constructed with many, many strands of very strong steel. Our lives are also constructed with many strengths. One of these strengths is our addiction. Life, like this cable, stretches out in front of us. The strands of steel are tightly intertwined, as is our addiction. The strands of steel, like our addiction, run the length and are with us to the end. When we are on the cable, we are in constant contact with the strands whether we realize it or not. If we traverse with only the cable, supporting us, the cable has all the power; we are powerless over what happens."

LOGISTICS

As each group member steps up to the cable, group members ask, "What addiction supports you?" The individual indicates his/her substance of choice (e.g., cocaine, alcohol, prescription drugs). As the individual steps up onto the cable, he/she is asked by the group, "Who has control? Do you have the power to make it?" The element or physical structure should be too unstable to remain on alone (i.e., cable or ropes should have some "give" to it/them.) Once the individual is standing on the ground again, the group asks, "Are you powerless over your addiction?"

As each member approaches the cable, he/she dialogues the following: "I admit I am powerless over alcohol. My life is unmanageable. I need help." Group responds: "We are powerless too; we will help you." Group members "spot" individual across cable (group should know basic "spotting" technique).

DEBRIEFING

"If this cable truly has the power to control, perhaps we can manage it somehow. What way could you manage it alone?" Here, the therapist engages the group in suggestions. Each suggestion, in turn, receives a real life attachment. For example, a group member might say: "We could get rid of the cable." The therapist could answer: "Would that be like ending life?" Or the group member might say: "I could run across it really fast," and the therapist might respond with "Would you potentially get hurt?"

"If we admit that we are powerless, that this cable which represents life is unmanageable, we've acknowledged our recognition that our substance abuse has control and power over us; we've acknowledged our inability to make it using our substance abuse as support and we've acknowledged that our addiction is tightly woven into our life traverse. How then do we make it across?"

PARADOX

If the addict admits to being powerless over his/her life process when his/her substance is in control, he/she gains power. The power to say, "I'm powerless," is power.

STEP TWO

"Come to believe that a power greater than ourselves can restore us to sanity."

The focus of this process is on the illusion of having all the answers, the tendency for being closed-minded, and the paradox of seeing that we are blind.

SET-UP

Illumination River. This consist of twelve 2x2's. Wooden planks, bandannas, or pieces of cardboard are placed at random across an imaginary river called "The River of Addiction."

SAMPLE PRESENTATION

"We stand at the edge of the River of Addiction. It is a fast-moving river and it goes on forever. When we are in it, we are carried along, our body and soul thrown into rocks and debris. At times it tosses us onto the shore, where we struggle to dry out. But rest is brief, for soon the river will rise and we will find we are back in it. We are powerless in the river. It dictates our journey. We are also blinded by the spray of the frigid waters. Like today, there may be a time when we find ourselves tossed on the shore. We notice that the shore on the other side meets a cliff. The climb looks extremely difficult, and we doubt our ability to make it. Yet as we dry out, we become aware of the hurt and pain the River of Addiction has caused us. We decide to traverse 12 rocks that cross the river. Remember the spray of the River of Addiction when we leave the shore, because its tremendous presence blinds us."

LOGISTICS

Note: "Rounds" of this activity are conducted, the first when each group member attempts the River of Addiction by themselves, and the second with the verbal aid of other group members. In the first round, as each group member steps up to the edge of the River of Addiction, a blindfold is placed over his/her eyes (please follow your own policies and procedures for using blindfolds. Emotional and physical safety is the number one priority). Group members ask the person to identify their River of Addiction (i.e., what substance does the river contain?).

They are instructed that each time they step off the 2X2's they will start over. As they step out, group members remain silent. The therapist asks individuals to verbalize their awareness and feelings. Words like "frustrated," "confused," and "unbalanced" should emerge. Allow each individual to attempt crossing the River of Addiction alone. Repeat above process for each.

In the second round, as each member approaches the 12-rock crossing, he/she is blindfolded and the group members verbally guide him/her across the River of Addiciton. He/she begins his/her crossing with the following statement: "I cannot make it alone." The group responds, "We are here to help you. We add to your power." The person crossing then says, "I now have a power greater than myself."

DEBRIEFING

"Was there a sense of insanity out there? A sense of being out of control? A sense of not being able to get there alone? What can restore you, take that frustration away? Are you willing to allow something greater than you alone to help you make it? Are you willing to see that you are blinded by your addiction and cannot make it there on your own?"

PARADOX

Once the group responds, the addict "sees" that his/her addiction has blinded him/her. He/she is illuminated and begins to see the way.

STEP THREE

"Make a decision to turn our will and our lives to the care of God as we understand him."

The focus of this activity is on a Higher Power as the processes of trust, leaving the substance behind, and of experiencing the reality of serenity emerge.

SET-UP

Letting Go. A traditional trust fall set-up is used. The trust fall ladder is preferable to a platform because it is narrow and less stable. In addition, the presence of a pole or tree to wrap an arm around is important (follow your policies and procedures for trust falls). As with the last activity, two "rounds" of the experience are conducted, each with an introductory frame.

FIRST SAMPLE PRESENTATION

"The process of letting go is a process that begins with recognition of fear. Fear tells us to hold on. Fear hastens us to find relief. Fear reminds us that we are afraid. The pole is our substance, what we grab onto when we feel fear. It is always there. In fact, letting go is attached to it."

LOGISTICS OF THE FIRST ROUND OF THE ACTIVITY

Each group member climbs to the fall platform or ladder rung without the spotters in position. Group members have not yet been instructed on trust fall procedures. He/she verbalizes the sensations, and feelings that occur while he/she holds onto the pole or tree. Group members ask individuals what they are holding onto. Group members ask individuals what they are afraid to let go of.

PRESENTATION AND LOGISTICS OF THE SECOND ROUND OF THE ACTIVITY

In the second round of the activity, group members are instructed in trust fall technique for climber and spotters (please follow your policies and procedures). An individual climbs to the ladder or platform alone. The following commands are used: "I want to turn over my will and my life. You can let go of (substance). I'm letting go" (individual falls). Group members remain nonverbal except for commands. Once the individual is in the group's arms, group members remain silent and gently "rock" the individual to the ground where they gently lay the individual down.

DEBRIEFING

"If we hang onto the pole, we can go nowhere. We may feel safe and secure, but we are extremely limited in our choices. Yet, we are well aware that if we let go, nothing will catch us. We need to be prepared to seek out a safety net if we are going to let go. Who or what becomes our safety net? We can let go of our substance and our fears and be safe. We may come to recognize that it is easier to let go then to hang on. Hanging on is exhausting and provides stress. Letting go is energizing and provides serenity."

PARADOX

In order for the addict to let go, he/she has to recognize what he/she has been holding onto.

STEP FOUR

"Make a searching and fearless moral inventory of ourselves."

The focus of this activity is a process on the gathering of trait information.

SET-UP

Trait Relate. This consists of a ring bungee that has ropes attached to it. The bungee ring is placed at center of 10'x10' roped off area. Attached ropes are long enough to reach out of the 10x10 area. Within the 10x10 area are blocks. Each block has one of AA's Seven Deadly Sins (pride, greed, lust, dishonesty, gluttony, envy, and laziness) printed on it. In addition, the Seven Necessary Virtues (humility, altruism, respect, honesty, moderation, trust, and motivation) are each printed on separate blocks and are buried beneath leaves or some other cover. Within the 10x10 area, place a garbage can on a stump.

SAMPLE PRESENTATION

"Within the boundaries of our life (e.g., home, work, and community) lie our assets and liabilities. Also, within the boundary of our lives is our addiction. When our addiction fills the boundaries of our lives, like the leaves within this roped area, our virtues are essentially buried, lost, difficult to find and take hold of. What is evident, however, is our liabilities. In fact, they become quite obvious. When others enter the boundaries of our life, they can't help but notice our liabilities and they would have to struggle to find our virtues."

LOGISTICS

Have members of the group attempt to read aloud the virtues printed on the blocks (this should be difficult because they should be hidden under leaves or some other cover). Then, have members read aloud the liability blocks, which should be bold and obvious.

DEBRIEFING

"In order to recognize our assets and liabilities, we must look for them. When we are within the boundaries of our addiction, like at home or at work or in our community, it is difficult. Often, we need to step out of our boundaries, like you have, by seeking treatment in order to find what lies within them. We begin our search with the help of others, others who are also searching. Together we assist one another in grabbing hold of ourselves. We identify a problem behavior as we gather a negative liability and then place it in the garbage can. We also gather virtues from beneath the leaves and verbalize new, positive behaviors. We place these virtues on a platform for all within our boundaries to see, above our addiction."

PARADOX

As the addict faces the negatives, he/she also reveals his/her essential goodness.

STEP FIVE

"Admit to God, to ourselves, and to another human being the exact nature of our wrongs."

The focus on this activity is the process of giving and receiving forgiveness.

SET-UP

Courage Walk. Set up this initiative like a trust walk. Divide group in half, giving one group blindfolds (please follow your policies and precedures and infection control guidelines for blindfolds).

SAMPLE PRESENTATION

"It takes great courage to admit our wrongs. With it comes the feeling of fear again. With fear comes that desire to hold onto our addiction and use it for support. Part of letting go is letting it out. As we stand now, dig deep and bring to the surface a wrong, a wrong you have not yet found the courage to admit. As long as you hold onto your addiction for support, it will block who you truly are. It will keep you blinded to the light of true freedom. You remain in the dark."

LOGISTICS

Have half the group put blindfolds on before they know who their partner will be. Ask entire group to remain nonverbal until further instructed. Ask the blindfolded individuals to verbalize their feelings and sensations as they stand before the group blindfolded. Ask them to recall a wrong without sharing. Have them describe how it feels to bring it to mind. Blindfolded members are led by a partner they cannot initially identify. This partner leads the blindfolded individual around safely until the blindfolded individual shares a wrong. It should be shared at some length. Once shared, the individual may remove the blindfold. The same sequence will be used until each group member has the blindfolded experience.

DEBRIEFING

"As wrongs fester inside of us, we call on alcohol and substances to cover up the associated feelings. It takes great courage to share our wrongs. When we do, the dark is lifted and good, positive, warm light fills the vacancy deep inside where the wrong used to live."

PARADOX

By admitting our wrongs, we make it right.

STEP SIX

"We are ready to have God remove all defects of character."

The focus of this activity is on commitment to continually let go of the need to control.

SET-UP

The Commitment. Set up Wild Woosey (Rohnke, 1989).

SAMPLE PRESENTATION

"These two cables are constructed with strands of steel. Like our addiction, they are tightly woven together and run throughout. The path of this cable represents the path of our recovery. When we initially stand on the cable, facing others that we are connected to in our lives, the cable provides the support. Our contact with another human being can be awkward and invasive."

LOGISTICS

Have group members pair up. As both climb onto the narrow end of the element, ask them to dialogue their awareness and feelings. Comments such as "awkward," "uncomfortable," "too close," and the desire to come down are often heard.

DEBRIEFING

"Our addiction continually drives us toward being in control. But here on the cable, as in addiction, the control is not ours. The cable dictates that in order to be in control we can go no further than standing here, hanging onto the pole, hanging on to our substance. To let go and make contact with another we have to let go. To let go and make contact with another we have to truly let go of our defect of character. As a result of devoting focus and energy to willingness, we make a commitment to give up and give in. As we move out on the cable, we become aware of being part of something bigger that is accompanied by a forward momentum. We form a partnership between ourselves as we develop an attitude of readiness and a Higher Power that supports and carries us there."

PARADOX

To gain, I must give up and give in.

STEP SEVEN

"We humbly ask Him to remove our short comings."

The focus of this activity is on rebirth as a surrender, as the experience of peace and serenity.

SET-UP

Rebirth Tire. This is a traditional ropes course event where a participant is passed through a tire or small space. If using rope instead of a tire, participants cannot grab on and crawl through alone.

SAMPLE PRESENTATION

"We stand before an opening, an opening that can lead us to a new beginning. In order to get through the opening, we have to stay within the boundaries. These boundaries represent a tradition, a tradition that guides us toward feeling safe and secure."

LOGISTICS

Have each group member dialogue about the truths they realize as they stand before the Rebirth Tire. "What truths do you recognize? How does humility help us see the truth?" The therapist wants to emphasize powerlessness to get through alone, availability of help, and the tendency for defects of character (e.g., pride) to keep us from moving through.

DEBRIEFING

"If we recognize and declare the truths, that we are powerless to get through alone, that we experience our character defects (e.g., I really want to get through on my own; I really do not want anyone to lift me), then we can move through with peace of mind. We are ready and we surrender in order to be born anew. This surrendering is not a loss, it is a win."

PARADOX

Through surrender, we win.

STEP EIGHT & STEP NINE

"We make a list of all persons we have harmed and become willing to make amends to them all."

"Make direct amends to such people, wherever possible, except when to do so would injure them or others."

The focus of this activity is on taking responsibility for relationships with others.

SET-UP

Amends Maze. Mark off a 10'x10' area. Members of the group position themselves in the area and remain still. One individual is the sponsor, the other is the addict. They stand opposite one another, across the area, with the other members in between.

FIRST SAMPLE PRESENTATION

"We are connected throughout our lives to all the individuals we have harmed. We cannot remove them. We may pretend they do not exist, but actually their presence blocks our movement forward."

LOGISTICS

The addict labels each individual in the area as a person they have "harmed." For example, "You are my mother, you are my son," etc. The gender of the person in the area does not matter.

SECOND SAMPLE PRESENTATION

"Now it is time to take the action needed to make amends. To acknowledge those who may have suffered the most from our destructive behavior we must black out external influence and look deep within ourselves. We must, in order to make amends:

1. Face each person and admit the wrong we have done.
2. Apologize sincerely.
3. Make whatever restitution we can.
4. Change our behavior to avoid causing the same harm again. Through this process we can move ahead."

LOGISTICS

The individual is blindfolded. His sponsor across the area now guides him toward each labeled individual (e.g., toward Mary whom the addict has labeled as "son"). Once standing in front of Mary, the addict asks, "Who are you?" Mary responds, "I am your son." The addict now admits a wrong he has done to his son, apologizes, tells "him" what restitution he will provide and identifies a "new" behavior that will not cause harm. Group members can assist the addict in remembering these steps, but only if he asks. When finished, he moves on to another, eventually reaching his sponsor, who represents abstinence.

PARADOX

Admitting wrongs makes them right.

STEP TEN

"Continue to take personal inventory and when we are wrong, promptly admit it."

The focus of this activity is on continutation, on active awareness along the way.

SET-UP

Recovery Traverse. A low "wall traverse" is used. At the base of the traverse, platforms are set at "rest" intervals. These represent "meetings along the way." Traverse should be low so that spotters are not needed. (Follow your policies and procedures for this event.)

FIRST SAMPLE PRESENTATION

"Recovery is ongoing, just like the River of Addiction. They are very close together; in fact, they meet. Through dishonesty with ourselves we can have one foot in recovery and one foot in addiction. But each time we touch down into the river, we've experienced relapse. Whether in the River of Addiction or on the Recovery Traverse we are connected to others. Our actions and reactions affect them."

LOGISTICS

As the group gets onto the wall traverse, they are connected together with a length of rope. They are asked not to communicate with one another, to "experience the isolation of trying to recover alone." Whenever someone steps down off the wall, the entire group returns to the beginning. Allow the group to verbalize the feelings that emerge: frustration, disappointment, anger, hurt.

SECOND SAMPLE PRESENTATION

"Recovery is continuous. That is why we are recovering, never recovered. Even though we may be abstinent from our substance, our addiction still flows through our life, much like the imaginary river that flows along this "rock wall" or Recovery Traverse. Much like recovery we must hang onto certain things in order to continue on our recovery journey. We must be aware that our actions affect others, that we are indeed connected to others. We must realize that at times we need to rest, to take inventory, to assess our movement. And if we fall into the river, we must go back and begin again, to learn from our experience."

LOGISTICS

Return to wall traverse. Encourage individuals to be open, honest, and helpful in their needs. How can group members assist one another in traversing without relapse? How can the rest or "meeting" platforms be used to take inventory and assess the process of the journey?

PARADOX

Moving slow makes faster progress.

STEP ELEVEN

"We seek through prayer and meditation to improve our conscious contact with God as we understand him, praying only for knowledge of His will for us and the power to carry that out."

The focus of this activity is on meditation as having no boundaries, as involving centering and focus.

SET-UP

Centering Climb. Use the traditional pamper pole set-up. (Please follow your policies and procedures for this event. Emotional and physical safety are the number one priority.)

SAMPLE PRESENTATION

Have members verbalize what limitations they perceive in experiencing the pamper pole event. Where will they get stuck? Then, have group members verbalize the limitations they perceive in their recovery process. "The idea of prayer and meditation may have you struggling. If we've never experienced spiritual awakening, we have no information on how it will feel.

Our addiction cannot maintain control if we move beyond the limitations it presents. It cannot control if we climb beyond the point where it tells us to stop. This is a spiritual awakening. Moving beyond limitations. How do we move beyond limitations? First we have to identify them."

LOGISTICS

Individual members experience the pamper pole event. In order to begin their process, the individual climber must ask the group members to prepare him/her. Group members prepare the climber with equipment. The therapist remains silent here, allowing the individual to turn himself/herself over to the higher power of the group. (NOTE: Staff is ultimately responsible for climber's safety. Follow all guidelines.) Individual begins climb with the following commands: "I am prepared to focus, to climb beyond my addiction."

DEBRIEFING

"How can meditation move you through these limitations. How can focus give you the power to climb higher? What knowledge can the higher power of the group provide the individual climbing? How deep down do we have to focus and how far out do we have to reach?"

PARADOX

Through focus we broaden our perspective.

STEP TWELVE

"Having had a spiritual awakening as the result of these steps, we try to carry this message to addicts and to practice these principles in all our affairs."

The focus of this activity is on moving to a position where we can assist others in their challenge.

SET-UP

Looking ahead, looking back. Traditional "initiative wall" (Rohnke, 1989). (Please follow your policies and procedures for this event.)

SAMPLE PRESENTATION

"As addicts we stand in front of the wall of addiction and believe we can climb it alone. We try, we fall, we get hurt. We try harder, we become frustrated. The wall is in control, yet we refuse to see what it has done to us.

With assistance, we move onward and upward, yet we are always aware of the wall of addiction that we face. It is always there, in front of us; that hasn't changed. By accepting others' help, we are given the power to stay above our addiction. By reaching out to help others, we keep our addiction at arm's length. What hasn't changed is the presence of our walls; what has changed is the way we experience them."

DEBRIEFING

"Could anyone in this group get up this wall unassisted? Why would that be difficult? Can we recover unassisted? Does this ever change? What changes?"

PARADOX

Nothing has changed, yet everything has changed.

CONTRIBUTOR

Juli Lynch, MS
Odyssey Program
215 Caernarvon Road
Wales, WI 53183, USA
(414) 968-2348

THE WALL AND THE ADDICTION BACKPACK

INTRODUCTION

This initiative was designed for adolescents participating in a school-based Sobriety Support Group (SSG). Each participant and the group accepted the challenge of climbing The Wall initiative while wearing individual backpacks. The backpacks serve to represent the addiction each participant possesses and will continue to carry throughout life. To further develop the metaphors, items were placed in each backpack that signified possible characteristics of each individual's addiction.

The conditions for acceptance and participation in the SSG were participation in a weekly, after-school Alcoholics Anonymous group and 30 continuous days of sobriety (individuals had recognized and accepted their substance abuse addiction problem). Student participants and the substance abuse counselor had worked together as a group and individually for a significant period of time. The elements of the Full Value Contract had been embraced.

GOALS

Several characteristics of an addiction are emphasized during the initiative brief and highlighted during the processing. They include: (1) Each individual's addiction will be with them throughout their life;(2) the addiction can continue to have a detrimental influence on a person's life or can be positively redirected; and (3) the degree of presence of the addiction and its characteristics are variable.

SET-UP

Model the basic set-up as well as safety guidelines of this initiative after The Wall as outlined in *Cowstails and Cobras II* (Rohnke, 1989) except for the addition of backbacks and the contents you select. The following contents have been used:

1. Balloons that will hopefully pop to represent that relapse may be eminent.
2. Fifteen pound bag of sand to represent the nagging persistent presence of the addiction.
3. Tangled twine analogous to a feeling of confusion.
4. Nerf balls to represent bouncing back from a relapse.
5. Pots and pans to signify "too many pots in the fire."

Add anything that you think represents a characteristic of the addictions of the participants in your Sobriety Support Group. The substance abuse counselor can give the appropriate backpack to the appropriate participant to increase the likelihood of metaphoric transfer.

The backpack itself can represent a pack of beer or the persistent presence of the addiction. The person with the backpack containing balloons should put the pack on their chest to increase the likelihood of the balloons popping. Another possibility in the set-up is that the participants can be blindfolded to represent their addiction or the difficulty asking for help in controlling their addiction.

SAMPLE PRESENTATION/LOGISTICS

"Each of you has been given an 'addiction backpack' with contents that represent specific characteristics of your addiction at this time in your life. Look at and think about the contents of your backpack. You must carry your packs throughout this climb just as you will always carry your addiction. Since your addiction began, it has caused problems and difficulties in your life. Remember, however, that you must now think of ways your addiction can help you. Your addiction will always be present.

The goal of this climb is for the entire group to climb over the wall using only yourselves and your addictions to help. Once someone has climbed the wall, neither they nor their addiction can help another climber. Anyone and everyone must spot each other. For safety reasons the following rules must be followed:

1. Only one person can climb the wall at a time.
2. Each person must be spotted until they are completely over the wall.
3. No one can be held head first from the top of the wall."

DEBRIEFING

The primary focus of the debrief should be to encourage each participant to articulate what the backpack and the associated contents represent for them in reference to their addiction. Subsequently, ask the participants to add any thoughts concerning the significance of any of the contents for them or another participant. Several of the metaphors that members of the Sobriety Support Group have relayed are:

1. *Tangled Twine*: The recovery process from an addiction is similar to knots that are difficult to untie.
2. *Backpack*: The addiction is easy to forget but is always present. The characteristics of the addiction can change just as trading the contents in a backpack can change.
3. *Balloons*: The popping balloons are similar to brain cells dying, passing out, and falling over the edge. Relapse sometimes occurs when you want it to and when you don't want it to, similar to being unable to predict when a balloon might pop.
4. *Nerf Balls*: The light weight of the nerf balls represents using the Sobriety Support Program and the addiction to your benefit.
5. *Blindfolded*: Most people are blind to their addiction and have difficulty asking for help and acknowledging their feelings. While being blindfolded, you can continue to feel left out and remain in self-pity.
6. *Pots and Pans*: Because many different pots are in the fire, you cannot focus on the problems associated with your addiction.

Remember to ask if the group used their addictions in any way to help each other climb the wall.

CONTRIBUTOR

Andy Greif
Experiential Education Coordinator
Andrea DiBenedetto, Social Worker
Sobriety Support Group Participants, Fall '91
Windham R.E.A.L. School
Windham, ME 04043, USA
*(207) 892-4462

MOHAWK TRAVERSE

INTRODUCTION

This metaphor, which involves the Mohawk Traverse, can be used with chemically dependent/dually diagnosed adults and adolescents. With this metaphor, each tree (or however your Mohawk is constructed) represents an additional 30 days clean. (For example, tree number one is zero, tree number two is 30, tree number three is 60.) A fall off the cable represents a relapse and the entire group starts over again. Depending on the functional level of the group, the requirement for the entire group to start over can be modified. However, we prefer that the entire group start over to reinforce that an individual relapse has an effect beyond that individual (e.g., family, peers). Regardless of how the metaphor is implemented, please remember to follow all standard safety procedures.

GOAL

Identify individual and group behaviors that affect recovery in a positive or negative way. Identify underlying feelings associated with a relapse or with working through recovery.

LOGISTICS

Mohawk Traverse
Group Size: Five to 16 participants

SAMPLE PRESENTATION

"Sometimes being in recovery can feel like a tightrope or balancing act. Going too far to the edge or leaning too far to one side can have unpleasant consequences. This event is called the Mohawk Traverse, but today it represents your tightrope act. You have to use your creativity, imagination, and intelligence because this is intense training to help you prepare for the rigors of recovery. Each tree represents another 30 days clean; each time you fall off represents a relapse, and with each relapse the entire group starts over again. This is done to heighten your awareness of how a relapse affects more than just one individual. Your task is to get the entire group through recovery down to that last tree, which is 120 days clean and beyond.

DEBRIEFING

The debrief should address those behaviors and underlying feelings that helped people move through recovery or those behaviors and feelings that led to a relapse. The consequences and feelings surrounding a relapse should be discussed as well as what it felt like to move through recovery and get to 120 days clean and beyond. Issues such as support, asking for help, individuation, etc. can be addressed.

CONTRIBUTORS

Phil Ritchie, MS, CTRS
Director, Creative Therapy
Elmcrest Hospital
Portland, CT 06480, USA

Greg Gassner, MA
PhD Candidate
Sports Psychology
Temple University
Philadelphia, PA 19122, USA

SOBRIETY BALL

INTRODUCTION

This is an adaptation of the traditional event called Moonball. Its application is primarily for chemically dependent/dual diagnosis populations. In this scenario, the ball represents a person's sobriety.

GOAL

Identify individual or group tendencies that support or sabotage sobriety (e.g., attitudes, impulsiveness, selfishness).

LOGISTICS

Number of participants vary, but generally range from 5 to 16 in a circle formation.

One ball (e.g., a beach ball, an oversized soft-cover volleyball) that is fairly large and does not present a safety concern for fingers, wrists, etc. is needed.

SAMPLE PRESENTATION

"Today you're going to be involved in an event using this ball, which could represent your sobriety. Now you have to use your intelligence, creativity, and imagination because this event is intense training for the challenges you will face once you're discharged from the hospital. The challenge for today is to see how well you will take care of your sobriety. The way that we're going to be able to tell this is by counting the number of times that we hit the ball without letting it touch the floor. The higher the number, the more you are taking care of your sobriety. The lower the number, the more you are sabotaging your sobriety. The only rule that you have to remember is that one person cannot hit the ball twice in a row and you can only hit the ball with your hands. Any questions? Let's get started."

DEBRIEF

Debriefing questions should focus around the specific behaviors that supported or sabotaged people's sobriety. Underlying feelings connected with these behaviors should be explored and transferred to other situations in and out of the treatment setting.

Some paradoxical work can also be done with this event in that the ball can represent anger. In this scenario, you are asking group members to develop their anger. As this scenario plays itself through, a group member may slam the ball to the ground or out of the circle, not wanting to develop their anger any longer.

CONTRIBUTORS

Phil Ritchie, MS, CTRS
Director, Creative Therapy
Elmcrest Hospital
Portland, CT 06480, USA

Greg Gassner, MA
PhD Candidate
Sports Psychology
Temple University
Philadelphia, PA 19122, USA

MIRK'S RECOVERY

INTRODUCTION

Population: This activity is designed for people in a recovery program or other programs where skills/coping methods are learned and a return to a "hostile" environment is expected (e.g., returning to an old neighborhood after rehabilitating in some correctional environment).

Progression: This activity can be used when individuals have a working knowledge of what will be expected of them upon returning home/leaving treatment (e.g., aftercare planning, when an individual begins to assume the "I can handle it" excuse as a coping method). This activity seems to work best when an individual has begun to invest time and energy into the process of change and therefore will give maximum effort to guard the "cure" against those who wish to take it.

Contraindicating/Limiting Factors:

1. The facilitator should be aware of any physical limitations that would place the participant in a "no win" situation (e.g., if the participant has limited/deteriorated motor skills). If this is the case, the facilitator can place creative restraints upon the other group members to allow participants opportunities for success.

2. The facilitator should be aware of the overall aggressiveness of the group and their ability to abide by the activity guidelines. As is the case with some activities, there is an element of potential injury present and safety guidelines should be observed at all times.

GOALS

1. The reality of relapse and losing the gains made during the treatment/rehabilitation phase.
2. The feeling of isolation (Scenario 1) and of support (Scenario 2).

3. Processing these feelings with the group. Was the individual successful in defending the "cure"? If not, how do they deal with what happened?

SET-UP

Area: Logistics for this activity are simple. An area large enough to accommodate your group plus some additional space for moving around. The entire activity will take place within a circle no larger than one that can be formed by your group standing one arm's length apart.

Equipment: The facilitator needs some type of pouch to store the "cure." A bandanna, lunch bag, or clean sock does fine.

Safety: It is important that all safety guidelines be followed to prevent injury.

Physical Safety Guidelines: Freeze immediately upon being touched by Mirk. Do not jump/lunge toward Mirk (see physical distraction). Visual distractions are permitted. Physical distractions are not permitted (e.g., "take downs"). If frozen, a participant can remain there or back away from the activity area (determined by the facilitator before activity begins).

Emotional: Emotional considerations are the responsibility of the facilitator. Always brief your group on being aware of the emotional risks involved anytime you deal with a group, and stop the activity if it appears someone's emotional boundary is being violated.

SAMPLE PRESENTATION

"Mirk was an elf who, very early in life, was cursed by an evil witch. The curse made Mirk suffer for many years. The curse made Mirk unreliable, dishonest, and manipulative to the point where he frequently misled others in order to get his way. Although the curse affected Mirk's behavior, his heart remained pure and it began to break each time he did something that hurt other people. Poor Mirk suffered so terribly that at times he felt like it would be better for everyone if he locked himself in a room for the rest of his life. One day Mirk met an old wizard who told him about a group of elves who had been cursed by the witch and had found a cure which broke the witch's spell. Mirk searched day and night for this group of elves; he finally found them in a cave just beyond the city walls.

The elves warmly welcomed Mirk into the cave and began telling him their stories of how the witch's spell had cost them their friends, family, jobs, and possessions. The more Mirk listened, the more he realized that these elves were just like him and the more he wanted the cure which they had found. The elves explained to him that in order to obtain the cure, which would keep him free of the witch's power, he must first pass a series of personal challenges that would at times seem impossible and irrelevant. These challenges were required because the witch had found out about the group of elves and became enraged that they would dare challenge her power. The witch disguised goblins as elves. She wanted these elves to enter the cave and bring some of the cure back to her so she could create a more powerful potion. But, as we all know, a goblin's heart is full of coal, and when challenged with openness and honesty they will fail every time. Mirk understood and with the help of a wise old elf as a mentor began to accept the challenges one at a time. Finally, the day came when Mirk was given a pouch that contained a crystal from the wall of the cave. The other elves explained to Mirk that it was not the crystal itself that held the power of recovery, but the energy that the group brought into the cave that would keep him safe from the witch's power. The crystal would hold the energy by itself, but only for a short period of time. And, if Mirk wanted to stay free from the witch's power, he would have to return to the cave each night.

The challenge that now faces Mirk is to guard his recovery from the goblins and other elves controlled by the witch who have been commanded to steal his pouch when he enters the city. The game begins when Mirk puts down his pouch momentarily to help another elf and looks up to find himself surrounded by the witch's goblins. Mirk cannot pick up his pouch because he needs both hands to fend off the goblins, but he stays as close as possible and does the best he can. Mirk realizes that he has the power to freeze the goblins by touching them, and the only way to get out of the circle with the pouch is to freeze them one at a time."

Scenario 2: It may be helpful to build upon this sequence by reintroducing the wise old elf which served as Mirk's mentor in the cave as an ally in the city. In this case, both elves would be fighting the goblins while guarding both of their pouches.

LOGISTICS

You may want to label each person attempting to steal the cure as an earlier agreed-upon barrier/obstacle that will be faced by the participant

(Mirk) upon leaving treatment (e.g., abusive spouse, unsupportive family, old friends, specific situations or places).

DEBRIEFING

There are several metaphorical associations in the story of Mirk. The curse is a metaphor for the problem of addiction; the personal challenges are metaphors for the work that must be done in a recovery program; the mentor is a sponsor; returning to the cave is continuing a regular meeting schedule; and entering the city that is full of goblins will be a challenge Mirk will face. As the game begins, a participant can begin to recognize some of the pressures he/she will face upon leaving the group setting and returning to an old neighborhood. Manageability, self-reliance, reliance on another (Scenario 2), and dealing with failure (loss of the pouch) are some issues that become evident as the game progresses.

This is but one interpretation of the story, and the issues that will arise from the participants cannot be predicted. Rather, they are to be experienced as the game evolves.

CONTRIBUTORS

Jay McLeod
Excel Program
The Springs
P.O. Box 467
Rockmart, GA 30153, USA
(800) 868-5468

Noland White
Boland Building
Central State Hospital
Milledgeville, GA 31062, USA
(912) 453-6866

REENTRY

INTRODUCTION

This initiative is designed for patients who are health care providers suffering from addictive and affective disorders. As patients prepare to leave the residential treatment component of their recovery and return to their community, they report anxiety regarding their ability to maintain plans for their recovery programs.

The initiative is best utilized when: (1) participants have had a previous history of group process together, (2) the group is knowledgeable on spotting techniques, (3) participants are experiencing the termination phase of their treatment or group process, (4) participants are preoccupied with relapse or fear of not following their recovery plan outside of a therapeutic setting, and (5) participants are having difficulty separating their self-concept from the disease concept of addiction, evidenced by reporting the experience of feeling shame after mood shifts or by feeling anger at oneself for becoming addicted.

GOALS

The initiative will create an opportunity for participants to: (1) identify the coping skills of maintaining focus on a goal or recovery plan; (2) differentiate personal responsibility from that of peer support; and (3) deal with fear of relapse by experiencing an altered mood or state with associated feelings among peer support without violating abstinence or recovery plan.

SET-UP

The initiative traditionally called Balance Broom is utilized. Six or more participants are ready to spot, while standing in a circle, and are prepared to intervene on a fall from an individual in the center. The spotted individual holds a dust broom straight up, with arms extended, and proceeds to spin around the broom 15 times. After the spinning participant gives a signal that s/he is ready to stop, s/he drops the bristle side of the broom to the ground and attempts to step over it while holding on the other end with one hand. Spotting continues until the individual indicates s/he is able to stand on his own.*

SAMPLE PRESENTATION

"The next activity is called Reentry. If you choose to participate, you may experience many of the physical and emotional sensations inherent to reentry into your community as a recovering human who also works as a health care professional. Like the cyclic movement of shifts in a hospital or changing seasons, you may experience cycles in your recovery. The broom is meant to represent your program of recovery. During treatment, it's common to have a fairly good grasp and focus on recovery. The goal of the Reentry challenge is to maintain your grasp on your recovery by holding the broom high over your head, rotate around it 15 times, and then let the broom fall and step over it while trusting your group to support you. Support from the group looks like spotting with verbal acknowledgement."

Spotting Commands:

Spinner: "ready to support?"
Spotters: "yes or no"
Spinner: "ready to live (spin)"
Spotters: "live (spin) on"
Spinner: "living (spinning)"
Spinner: if falling, "help"

Remember Guidelines:

1. Use commands and wait for acknowledgement of support.
2. Hold your program (broom) high with your arms fully extended.
3. Step over your program (broom) when you're done spinning.
4. Remember you are responsible for communicating your limits to ensure your safety.

LOGISTICS

Two facilitators are recommended to ensure adequate spotting. Frequently, the group will spot adequately until the spinner has stepped

---

*Do not allow anyone with a history of seizures to participate by spinning.

over the broom and then they quit with the assumption that the initiative is over. The spinning participant usually remains disoriented for one or two minutes after attempting to step. It is necessary for the facilitator to encourage spotting until the participant has given verbal acknowledgement of stability.

The broom must be monitored and spotted by a facilitator to decrease chances of spotters getting hit by it when it falls. The spinner may need to be reminded to maintain a handhold on the end of the broom after it drops.

Frequently, the spinning participant may not wish or be able to complete 15 rotations. The participants' discovery of a limit can be reframed as a boundary; boundary setting is an additional tool of recovery. Participants who do not complete 15 rotations are still encouraged to attempt the step.

Important: Note that an alternative, possibly easier, version of this activity is for participants to spin around the broom rather than hold it high in the air. This is accomplished by placing the broom (or stick) on the ground and the other end on the participant's forehead. The participant also places one of her/his hands between the upper end of the broom stick and head (don't want anything impaled!). Once in this position they walk around the broom as quickly as possible 15 times.

DEBRIEFING

Participants often report that it is easier to complete rotations by maintaining a focus on an end of the broom; allowing eyes to wander during spinning results in increased dizziness and disorientation. The metaphor "It is easier to live in recovery if focus is maintained on a recovery program" often occurs in response to the question "What did you do to most effectively rotate?"

The isomorphs introduced in the mentioned spotting commands provide opportunities for additional metaphors regarding the responsibility of the individual to choose recovery prior to being open to help from support groups (e.g., have to choose to live in recovery before I am able to receive support in it). The metaphor is often accessed by the questions "What was the responsibility of the individual who rotated in relation to the group of spotters?" and "How is the responsibility of the individual similar to a newcomer in a support group?"

Many chemically dependent participants report an experience similar to a drug rush or panic when the broom falls and they attempt to step over it. The metaphor "If I disregard my program and relapse I will feel out of control" occurs in response to the questions "What feelings were experienced when letting the broom drop to step over it?" and "What metaphor does stepping over the program represent for you in your recovery?" It is important to process feelings associated with the rush. I like to reframe the experience into the idea that abstinence from an addictive behavior often results in opportunities for new experiences and feelings. Fear about reentry from a residential care setting to the patient's community is externalized as the participant remembers the support of spotters while discussing it.

Additional metaphors and isomorphs

1. One spin at a time.
2. Grabbing my program is a choice to recover.
3. Rotating or spinning represent living in recovery.
4. The broom represents the individual's plan for recovery (program).

CONTRIBUTOR

Mark J. Baumgartner, MEd, CADAC
Primary Counselor
Recovery Program for Health Care Professionals
Sierra Tucson
16500 N. Lago Del Oro Parkway
Tucson, AZ 85737, USA
(800) 624-9001

SWING TO RECOVERY (DISK JOCKEYS)

INTRODUCTION

This activity has been used with a chemically dependent group of adolescents ascribing to a 12-Step-recovery model. Group members are at different stages in treatment, so heterogeneity is a factor. Refusing help or assistance to others may not necessarily be bad; this behavior is evaluated on an individual basis given consideration of what's best for that individual at this point in treatment.

GOALS

1. Establish boundaries.
2. Reduce inappropriate thrill-seeking.
3. Gain control over impulsivity.
4. Increase insight to and understanding of issues in recovery.
5. Promote healthy risk-taking.

SET-UP

Utilize the traditional Disk Jockeys set-up with the following changes:

1. The area where the group begins is known as "Rehab."
2. The area beyond Rehab where disks lie is denoted as "Danger Zone."
3. Disks are denoted as one's "program" or "Circles of Abstinence."
4. If an individual contacts Danger Zone, he/she must return to Rehab.
5. Knocking over "trip wire" at start signifies a slip and the individual must return to Rehab.

SAMPLE PRESENTATION

"This activity is called The Swing to Recovery. You are all trying to achieve abstinence. In this activity, this is accomplished by occupying a disk and working your program (occupying a disk known as a Circle of Abstinence). While here you are sober and in recovery. To get there, however, you will have to swing over an area known as the Danger Zone. This area is full of your old past, hangouts, partners, and habits, all those things that brought you to seek the destructive path you are now on. Anyone's recovery is very tenuous, constantly facing the risk of relapse, a relapse that could be your last, leading to your death. There is no assurance you will ever be able to be sober again and continue your recovery. Contact with the Danger Zone is relapse. You will return to Rehab and, as noted, there is no assurance you will be able to success-fully swing to abstinence again. As you can see, just being close to it you run the risk of making that one fatal slip that may cost you your sanity.

You'll notice some of the 'Circles of Sobriety' are more in the middle of the Danger Zone than others. Working these programs is particularly hazardous in that you don't have as many supports around as you would occupying other circles. Should you be working a program from your position of abstinence and make contact with the Danger Zone, you must go back to Rehab and begin your recovery all over again. The difference this time is that the program you were working (i.e., the circle you had occupied) is no longer available. It is removed and you must seek a different path. This removal also exposes more of the Danger Zone. When embarking on your swing to recovery and abstinence, you must first alert others in recovery of your intentions to join them. Their support must be secured prior to your swing."

LOGISTICS

The Danger Zone may be strewn with props reflective of chemical substances.

DEBRIEFING

Keep the following in mind while debriefing:

1. Thoughtful consideration of the fragility of abstinence and the nature of the disease.
2. Explore the dichotomy of how helping others is necessary for the survival of the fellowship and AA, while at the same time may be detrimental to one's own recovery.
3. Identify behaviors helpful in recovery.
4. Identify behaviors which may impact negatively on sobriety.

CONTRIBUTOR

Philip Errico
Bonnie Brae Educational Center
Valley Road
Millington, NJ 07946, USA

A ROAD TO RECOVERY: A RELAPSE PREVENTION INITIATIVE

INTRODUCTION

This activity is based on a Minefield initiative. The object is for one participant to verbally guide another who is blindfolded from one side of the minefield to the other without touching them. Guidance through the minefield is accomplished using only verbal commands. No physical contact is permitted.

SET-UP

The boundaries of the minefield are roped off to form a funnel. The purpose of this is to have blindfolded participants come in physical contact with one another near the end of the minefield. This interaction can represent either: (1) the pressure of peers to engage in relapse activities or (2) the converse, where peers could help each other through the minefield. Participants can walk through the congested end of the minefield "train" fashion to help each other through. However, if they and their guides do not think through this solution, then someone will probably relapse by contacting a mine.

An important part of the set-up is for students to indicate their drugs of choice and the recovery tools they have or foresee accessing. Subsequently, students label these "relapse mines" and "recovery tools." One problem can occur when students see these mines and tools placed in the minefield, and the positions of these objects are not moved between the changing of roles from sponsor to participant. The result can be that several students walk through the minefield without the need for much guidance from their respective sponsors. Consequently, we recommend that the metaphor presentation take place out of sight of the minefield, and the participants be blindfolded to prevent studying the minefield. In addition, the objects should be moved between the students' changing of roles.

SAMPLE PRESENTATION

The boundaries of the minefield may represent the boundary between those individuals in the sobriety support group and their friends who are still using and abusing addictive drugs of choice.

Students have commented that they do not want the minefield to end, since they feel that there is no end to the recovery process and relapse is always possible. Maybe a way to incorporate this thought into the initiative would be to have the end of the minefield represent the first step in relapse prevention (e.g., the end of the first year of sobriety) or whatever goal the group or individual has established.

DEBRIEFING

Sometimes students and their sponsors do not seriously look at the recovery tools. As a result, participants are asked if this represents a token effort toward their accessing and using recovery tools.

CONTRIBUTORS

Andy Greif, Experiential Education Coordinator
Andrea DiBenedetto, Social Worker
Sobriety Support Group Participants
Windham R.E.A.L. School
55 High Street
Windham, ME 04062, USA
(207) 892-4462

RECOVERY ACTIVITIES

POPULATION

These activities have been used successfully in an adolescent treatment facility. Groups are generally open-ended, with new patients arriving or patients leaving due to an early discharge or completion of the 30–42 day program. Patients come mostly from New England and from Long Island, NY, and tend to represent a balanced cross-section of economic and social backgrounds. Activities are usually done during "recreation" time or off-grounds in a park setting. Most of these activities can be adapted for use indoors or outdoors. They can also be used by any age group in recovery familiar with the 12-Step Program.

ACTIVITY #1
Blob Tag

INTRODUCTION

This game is usually played after a series of ice-breakers and other tag games. It incorporates some physical movement and motivates patients to begin looking at AOD (alcohol and other drug) concepts. The game is appropriate for all ages and for people who can physically run or walk around.

GOAL

This game is meant to be a simple introduction without a lot of analyzing or debriefing. The goal is for participants to have fun, begin to talk about drug abuse, and know it's okay to remember good times as well as "flashbacks" and other not-so-pleasant times in their past. Teachable moments on issues of communication may also occur.

SET-UP AND PRESENTATION

Participants are asked to pretend they have just come home from being out late with friends. They decide to watch television and go into the family room. (At this point boundaries are established, with enough room for people to run around without running into each other.) An old black-and-white movie called "The Blob" comes on. As they sit there eating their popcorn and slowly dozing off, they begin to have flashbacks or a bad dream. The Blob (as designated by the facilitator) begins to come out of the television (to the participants).

"You cannot leave the room (boundaries) because you might wake up your family and get into trouble for being late. You also don't want to make them think you've relapsed. If the Blob slimes you (tags you), you then become part of it. The Blob can only slime you if it is whole. If you go out of bounds you are automatically slimed. Only the hands of people on the ends of the Blob can tag you. The last person not tagged becomes the new Blob."

LOGISTICS

1. As the group grows there is a tendency for mass confusion and for the Blob to split apart.
2. If it is a large group or if the Blob is too big to catch people, the facilitator can subdivide the Blob and create two Blobs.

DEBRIEFING

As mentioned, this activity could have a short debrief where participants are asked to share how they worked together or what might have worked better. Participants usually share stories of times they were high and "flipping out" and couldn't tell anyone. We discuss communication (e.g., Who was heard? Who felt left out? How could the team work better at listening to each other?). Facilitators can point out some observations at this time, but usually the group quickly moves on to a new activity.

ACTIVITY #2
Beam—Geographical Cures

INTRODUCTION

One concept often heard in treatment is "If only I lived there," "If only I wasn't here," "Next time it will be different," or "I just need to move away from these people, places, and things." While moving to another location may bring temporary relief to a person struggling with addictions, you always catch up with yourself! This activity is designed to open up discussion for participants about the topic of geographical cures. This activity is good to use once some level of trust and other touching activities have occurred.

GOALS

The goals of this activity are to build trust, communication, and decision-making skills. Also included is an opportunity for participants to metaphorically experience the outcome of a geographical cure. This often lays the groundwork for discussion to occur about personal experiences.

SET-UP

Participants are asked to identify a place they believe they could go where all their problems and addictions wouldn't bother them. This may be a fantasy or real place. The participants are then divided into two teams. Each team is placed on one end of a log or beam facing the other team. Each team is told they are "here" and that the other team is "there." The object of the game is to get your team from here to there. If anyone falls off, the whole group must start over. Depending on the developmental stage of the group, there may be a lot of frustration and lack of communication. This also is a good activity to help assess group processes. A time limit is good to set and can allow for further challenge. This should be based on the group size and functioning level.

DEBRIEFING

Once the activity is either successfully completed or time has run out, participants should circle up for a debrief. Participants should discuss processes, successes, failures, communication problems, etc. Also, the facilitator should ask participants if anything changed by them going to their imaginary spot. Did going "there" resolve anything? What are times in your life you attempted a geographical cure? Did it work? For how long? What needs to change for things to work? The group should be recognized for the successes in the activity and told that the exercise is meant to open the door for discussion. Getting from "here" to "there" is a success in the activity, but it's the motivation behind the move that needs to be highlighted.

ACTIVITY #3
Using the Compass as a Sponsor

INTRODUCTION

Adolescents tend to have a difficult time with authority figures (and rightly so in some cases). An integral part of recovery for most people does require having a sponsor (i.e., a person who provides direction and encouragement in alignment with the 12 steps and 12 traditions of AA). Because an addict is on their guard from their addiction, a sponsor can usually help provide information that will keep the person conscious of the actions that can prevent relapse. Because "the addict" within may want to be active, there is a struggle created, and the person in recovery might find themselves ignoring their sponsor's advice and sometimes relapsing.

This activity is designed to introduce the concept of a sponsor and to initiate a series of trust activities. I usually begin this activity and follow it up with blind trust walks with peers guiding. These activities, in conjunction with other trust-builders, help participants recognize times they have lost trust in others or themselves. It also allows participants to begin trusting themselves by being responsible for their peers' safety.

SET-UP

Each participant is given a compass. They are shown the basic parts of a compass and how to take a bearing through simple activities. Participants take a bearing off a tree, pole, etc. approximately 100 feet away. They are then asked to imagine themselves deep in the woods. Their destination is a mountain, but they can only see the tip of it through the trees. As they move forward towards the mountain, it disappears from view.

The goal is to reach the destination by walking a straight line toward the mountain without the compass. Each participant is asked to partner up with someone else. The participant is blindfolded and paired up with another person there only to act as a spotter. The blindfolded person is pointed toward the goal and then must walk on their own to the goal. In most cases, they end up way off track. Other participants need to be quiet during this activity, as the sound can cause the blindfolded person to swerve.

After each person has tried the activity, let them use the compass. They are not allowed to look at their destination.

DEBRIEFING

At this point a discussion can occur around sponsorship. What was the effect of having a compass (sponsor) they could rely on for direction? When they find themselves in a thickly wooded area (personal struggle) and can only see the tip of their destination (recovery), they need to depend on their compass (sponsor) and not follow their own addictive thoughts in getting lost (relapse).

Did people feel safe? I encourage participants to discuss times they followed addict thoughts versus advice from a friend or relative. How can they tie resistance to participation in treatment, acting out behaviorally, or denial to this activity? How does having a sponsor or other recovering people in your life help? Will people not in recovery, like friends, be your only support after treatment?

ACTIVITY #4
Trolley—Footprints of a Higher Power

INTRODUCTION

The concept of a Higher Power is difficult for many people to accept or look at, yet it also is an integral part of the 12-Step Program. The beauty of the 12 Steps is that a Higher Power can be self-designed. The purpose of developing this concept is to help the alcoholic or addict restore themselves to a place of sanity. Higher Power for some is the AA group itself. It may be a tree or a traditional idea of God. In any case, the concept has been the foundation for many people in recovery and has sometimes worked better than other forms of therapy. This activity introduces the concept of a Higher Power in a way that is gentle and non-obtrusive.

SET-UP

The materials needed are the constructed trolley. This consists of a plank of wood with rope straps (two of these are needed to complete a trolley). See *Silver Bullets* (Rohnke, 1984) to construct. I ask one of the participants to read the poem "Footprints" (see Sample Presentation).

After the reading, they are then asked to get from point A to point B as a team without falling off. Each time a person falls off, they have to add distance to the final destination. The group has 10–30 minutes (adjusted for distance) to reach the final point. Remind the group that communication and process are just as important as reaching their goal. I also remind them (as a group of recovery people) that we can represent each other's Higher Power and help "carry" each other to the goal of recovery.

DEBRIEFING

The debrief generally centers around process, communication, and decision-making. I ask how people identified with the concept of a Higher Power in their lives. I ask them to share times in their life when they were using and realized something or someone was "carrying" them through. It's fun to do this activity in the snow or on sand so they can look back and see the "footprints" of the trolley.

SAMPLE PRESENTATION

"FOOTPRINTS"

"One night an old man had a dream that he had died and gone to heaven, where he was given a chance to review the footsteps of his life. He looked down and noticed that all over the dark valleys and difficult places he had traveled there was only one set of footprints, but over the plains and across the beautiful mountains there were two sets of footprints as if someone had walked by his side.

He turned to the Lord and said, 'There is something I can't understand about my life on earth. Why is it that across the mountains and over the smooth plains and easy places you have walked by my side, but here over the rough and difficult places I have walked alone, for I see in these places there is just one set of footprints?'

The Lord turned to the man and said, 'It is true that while your life was easy I walked along by your side. I was your companion; but here when the walking was hard and the path was difficult, here where you crossed the battlefields of life and did not have the strength to endure, I realized that that was the time you needed me the most.

And that is why I carried you.' "

CONTRIBUTOR

Robin Rieske
State of Vermont Human Services
P.O. Box 2483
West Brattleboro, VT 05303, USA
(802) 254-6222

GETTING THROUGH EARLY RECOVERY: AN ADAPTABLE METAPHOR

INTRODUCTION

I was originally exposed to this initiative as a potential exercise for management training/team building while at an advanced workshop at Project Adventure. I have left out a component of that exercise and simplified the initiative so that it can be used in a single session (60–90 minutes). The exercise can be used for any group of 4 to 12 participants (although 5 to 8 may be ideal). It is probably more appropriate for high school or older groups because of the difficulty of the initiative. I have used it mostly with adolescents at Spofford Hall, an inpatient chemical dependency/12-Step rehab hospital. The activity does not require strength or significant physical risk and can be done indoors or out.

GOALS

This initiative emphasizes communication, cooperation, group problem-solving/decision-making, attention to boundaries, honesty, and role-taking. For 12-Step programs, there is plenty of opportunity for the group to be reminded of AA slogans such as "Keep it simple" and "Easy does it." When groups have gotten stuck after the first step, I have sometimes suggested to the group that "If it works once, try doing it again." The idea of repeating a successful behavior or strategy is something that can be helpful in early recovery. The overall goal for participants to realize is tasks appear impossible (like staying sober) but are surmountable if they use their resources, strive for group unity (the first tradition of AA), and are patient with themselves.

SET-UP

The set-up for this activity is the Acid River/Meuse activity. This activity requires that the activity be set up before the group begins. Props required are at least seven cinder blocks (or blocks of equivalent sizes), three 2"x6"x8' boards and two ropes to designate the start and finish. The following diagram may help visualize the set-up. It is important to space the blocks so that a board can only reach between blocks in the same row (e.g., between AX and BX, CX and DX, and FX and GX), but not diagonally, such as from AX or BX to CX, or from DX to FX, or from FX or GX.

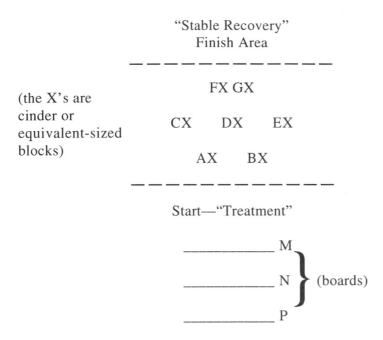

"Stable Recovery"
Finish Area

(the X's are cinder or equivalent-sized blocks)

FX GX

CX   DX   EX

AX   BX

Start—"Treatment"

M
N } (boards)
P

SAMPLE PRESENTATION

Before doing the activity, I start with a briefing that may include a review of group expectations, especially in terms of physical and emotional safety. A briefing may include safety considerations, rules of the game, and a framing of the intended learning experience. One way I have done this activity is to ask the group what issue they are working on in treatment. The group may identify getting along, dealing with anger, trust, sobriety, or (in this case) relapse shortly after leaving treatment. Once the participants (or the facilitators, if they know the group well enough) have identified a theme, then a name for the group metaphor emerges, such as "Getting over Anger," "Building Trust," "Avoiding Relapse," or (for the sake of example) "Getting Through Early Recovery." I tell the participants to think of things that get in the way of the issues on which they are working. For instance, if relapse has been identified as the treatment issue, then participants are each asked to identify at least one relapse trigger (e.g., if the issue was anger, then they would identify what makes them especially angry). Next the group is told that the ground between the two lines (dashed lines in picture) in the initiative (often designated by ropes) is an area where all the triggers they identified exist. I tend to walk around in this area naming all the relapses they have identified. I talk about the fact that when they first leave treatment, they will be exposed to all sorts of these obstacles.

Behind the line they are safe (in treatment, for hospitalized patients), but the place where they want to be and where they will have learned to manage their identified issue is past the far rope. In order to get from "here to there," the group has been given three tools. They are the three boards, which may represent their tools of recovery. Again, some framing about how the tools of recovery may be utilized can be suggested.

The group task is to find a way to get from treatment to a more stable recovery without making contact with any of the relapse triggers. The blocks serve as aids in their recovery. At this point, I ask individuals to identify what the blocks could represent. "What will be helpful to avoid relapse?" This way they have identified potential resources (e.g., AA meetings) in their recovery. Again, I tend to walk around identifying blocks as the resources they have mentioned.

For the purposes of the activity, the group is told that the blocks cannot be moved. If any of the boards touch the "relapse" area (the ground), then that board is contaminated and must be returned to the beginning for treatment before it can be reused. I emphasize that for safety reasons, no jumping is allowed during the activity. The activity is completed when all group members have safely entered the Stable Recovery Area with all the tools of recovery in hand and have congratulated one another.

Finally, if I know the group or certain participants well, I might assign them specific roles to experience. For instance, I have observed bright participants who tend to discover solutions to initiatives easily and dominate the problem-solving. I have assigned such participants to be silent ("a day of awareness" we call it) or told them they are only allowed to say certain things like, "I like what you just said/did."

SOLUTION

The most common solution I have seen work is when the group lays a board between block AX and BX and then lays a second board from the middle of the first board to block DX This is often where the group gets stuck and where I might make the comment above about repeating something that is working. Facilitators are strongly encouraged to work out the solution on their own before providing the activity for others.

ROLE OF THE FACILITATOR

Patience is critical for facilitators during this activity because a group may get stuck and frustrated and will usually get to the solution through moments of creative and rational emergence. If the group needs assistance (if facilitators think success is important for the group at that time), then I may inject some positive support of behavior that I think is beneficial to the group, both in terms of dynamics as well as toward the solution.

The group is assisted without disempowering them with too much help or direction. Being stuck can also be a dynamic within the group. I prefer to assist the group by helping them address possible dynamics that are surfacing if they show receptivity to my wonderings about what may be occurring. Otherwise, I leave it for the debriefing.

DEBRIEFING

If I have framed the initiative adequately at the beginning of the experience, then the debriefing can be quite short, almost as a review of whether the group experienced any connections between the original framing and their experience of the activity. I also use the debrief to address individual dynamics. For instance, if someone has been especially passive or controlling, or was assigned a particular role, I might ask that person and/or the group how they experienced that particular group member. I will also ask about certain events that occurred during the activity that may be worthy of addressing. For instance, while a group was doing the initiative, a board touched the ground. Almost immediately, a group member stepped off the board he was standing on into the relapsing area instead of considering his options. I raised a question as to whether his behavior was usual or unusual for him. He immediately stated how he tends to give up when something goes wrong and does not take time to assess the problem and potential options. We talked about how such a pattern might affect his recovery. I tend to raise events I noticed during the activity as simply things that I noticed and wondered about. If the individual or group is receptive, I may offer an interpretation or a connection to other behaviors or recovery issues I have noticed.

CONTRIBUTOR

Peter Lique-Naitove, EdM
7 Cobb Street
Keene, NH 03431, USA
(603) 357-8364

THE WILD WOOSEY AS A WAY TO DEMONSTRATE TRUST IN A METHOD: A METAPHOR FOR ACCEPTANCE OF THE AA WAY

INTRODUCTION

The Wild Woosey low challenge course element has traditionally been useful for experiencing intense interpersonal trust. In a setting such as a 12-Step Recovery Program, it is important to develop some trust in the AA process, something that can be foreign and often counterintuitive for the alcoholic. Add the usual opposition and defiance of a struggling adolescent and it is often difficult, if not impossible, to get a message through. As in the example below, I have found that adolescents can experience how they will rely on their usual way of doing things despite suggested alternatives. The participants are offered an opportunity to do their own thing in the face of suggestions, and then to try the suggested method for being successful in the activity.

GOALS

The goal of this low element is to provide a metaphoric experience of how it can be beneficial to accept/trust the "teachings" of a method in order to be more successful in one's efforts. The hope is that this will result in an increased receptivity to treatment and/or the AA 12-Step approach to recovery.

SAMPLE PRESENTATION

In this version of doing the Wild Woosey, I explain that the objective of the activity is for two people to work together, one on each of the diverging cables, so that the partnership can go as far as possible along the cables. I tell group participants that I am going to talk to them about how to be the most successful doing the activity. I also tell them that, although I will describe how to do the activity, they probably will choose not to follow my directions. I tell them that as they move down the cable they will want to try to keep their balance, by standing on the cable, holding onto each other, and bending over at the waist. I let them know that this is the usual way people go about trying this activity. A way to get farther down the cable is by working together. If they trust one another, lean into each other, keep the body stiff and arms high and straight, and push into the cable with their feet, instead of trying to stand on the cable, they will get farther. I also remind them that this is not the way they will do the activity on their first attempt. I tell them that they will get more than one opportunity to try the element. Before starting the activity, I also review spotting and explain what is required for spotting between the cables.

LOGISTICS

When participants first attempt the element, I say very little. On the second attempt, I am more active and help remind participants to straighten up by keeping their hips straight if they are bending at the waist and raising their hands higher and straighter as they go. I also encourage the partnership to make eye contact and work with one another. Peers will often begin to coach one another as I have modeled.

DEBRIEFING

I keep the discussion short and succinct. I ask if participants noticed any differences in their first and second (or more) attempts. I ask them to describe what seemed to work and what did not. Groups are often impressed with how far they advanced on the cables in an activity that first looked impossible. I ask them if they can see a connection between what they did on the activity and what they need to do in their recovery work. Often they identify the trust in themselves, others, and the ideas/methods that are being suggested to them (i.e., AA "teachings"). I suggest that they make a "mental snapshot" of what they were able to accomplish in this activity and that they can call on this mental picture when they are not feeling open to the ideas and suggestions of their treatment program.

CONTRIBUTOR

Peter Lique-Naitove, EdM
7 Cobb Street
Keene, NH 03431, USA
(603) 357-8364

FUNERAL FOR A FRIEND

INTRODUCTION

This metaphoric activity focuses on life from the death perspective. The activity was previously used in a group consisting of 10 "at risk" adolescent students and three staff with counseling backgrounds, but other populations may also benefit. The objectives of the group's 76-day wilderness stress challenge course consisted of developing basic independent living skills, improvements in self-concept, and enhanced social skills.

Before introducing the sensitive topic of death, some general rapport was developed among staff and students through various group adventure and focused discussion activities. The group had completed eight days of "Immersion," an 11-day introduction to backpacking, canoeing, rock climbing, stress-challenge, drama activities, and social skills development games. The evening activity took place while the group was camping next to an old cemetery that was adjacent to a wild onion field. A clear and warm full-moon night completed the scene.

Rapport among the group was now judged (informally by the staff and group) as generally open, honest, and fun, but also maniacally supportive and aggressively defensive in stressful and off-guard situations. Defensive behaviors were typical, such as derogatory criticisms, name-calling, or cursing. Little overt self- and other-valuing existed. Furthermore, the staff suspected, from the lack of related conversation among the youth, that there was little experience in death education and processing of emotions common to death (guilt, denial, anger, bargaining, depression, and acceptance).

GOALS

The goals of the activity followed the above mentioned needs: (1) to encourage positive support-valuing interactive behaviors, and (2) to better understand, accept, and positively utilize in the present the past or future experience of either one's death or someone else's death to improve inner and interrelationship behaviors.

SAMPLE PRESENTATION

Staff warmed the group up to conversation regarding death and checked for extreme sensitivities about death among the group. "The loss of someone close can be rough to deal with. But, perhaps we can also turn the experience into something positive. Maybe we can learn from the grief, anger, guilt, and sorrow that are experienced and also learn some important things about ourselves and the way we value others."

To gain some insight into the sensitivities of the group, and promote dialogue and support, staff asked everyone to speak, if comfortable, about any recent experiences of the death of close or loved ones. Staff and students carefully listened and shared similar experiences and feelings. Individuals were encouraged to participate only if they felt okay about it. After each of the group shared in turn, each person was asked to talk about the kind of funeral they would want and what it would represent about them. Staff encouraged creativity and suggested some positive images (e.g., the jazz procession in New Orleans). Finally, staff asked the followings questions: "If you died, how would you want others to remember you? How do you want to act towards others while they and/or you are alive?"

With this emotion/thought held within each individual, the group proceeded from the campsite to the onion field. By now, the group was assessed as quiet, reflective, and moving respectfully with each other. They seemed ready for some synergistic activity. Before beginning the main event, they held hands and meditated/prayed for strength to act with this energy and share it with the world.

LOGISTICS

Given space to walk about 20 paces in each "mini-funeral," each person either played dead or as a pallbearer in Funeral for a Friend. The pallbearers gently trust-lifted their "passed-on-friend" on their shoulders, walked slowly for about 20 paces, and held their "dead one" still for about 30 seconds. The bearers were instructed to think about how they would want to have treated (lifted, supported, comforted) their actual friends while they were alive. As a safety precaution against unexpected and clinical guilt, the bearers were also instructed not to dwell on any negative behaviors they might have done in the past. The "dead" were instructed to imagine themselves as dead, to relax completely and restfully, but able to review past behaviors and accomplishments as they were carried and held by "close friends and relatives." One student asked the bearers to hum "Amazing Grace." Staff supported, coordinated, participated, spotted, and gave thinking/feeling cues and reminders as the activity proceeded.

DEBRIEFING

After everyone had their chance to be dead, students were asked to share feelings, thoughts, and other reactions. Guilt, love, and fears about death were processed. The group provided individuals with valuable insights on how to think about or deal with death. The exercise also brought out the sharing of various everyday positive, supportive, comforting behaviors that now seemed even more important when viewed from the death perspective. The idea of "seizing the moment" seemed more crucial when viewed from the death or "opportunity lost" perspective. Choices and values were discussed concerning loving behaviors versus defensive and aggressive exchanges. Situations where each may be appropriate and powerful were discussed and differentiated. Causes of death related to these behaviors were suggested.

Finally, the cemetery was visited at around midnight in the full moon, after the group discussed respecting the actual dead as they would want to be respected. The presence of several children and family graves in the cemetery further drove home the point to "seize the moment." Various inscriptions were studied, with students encouraged to find one they'd like for themselves.

Death may offer a focused experience about the values and choices of everyday behaviors and relationships. While it may be a sad and painful experience, it can also teach us to better enjoy our living opportunities. The reactions were positive from all who participated. Behaviors seemed to change for the better, but periodic reminders were helpful and needed. In similar situations, student reactions may point out critical needs for more focused counseling in present or other settings.

CONTRIBUTOR

Timothy Francis, PhD, CTRS
11309 Gainsborough Road
Potomac, MD 20854, USA

CELEBRATING COMPLETION OF "GROUP"

SETTING

The setting is a therapy group for people with head injuries (i.e., six to 10 people meet weekly for a 90-minute therapy group, co-facilitated by a neuropsychologist and independent living staff).

GOALS

To provide support, explore feelings associated with loss, and understand the impact of a brain injury on psycho-social characteristics. Participation usually lasts one to two years. Different people graduate (terminate) and join throughout the year.

When a graduation is decided, that individual is asked to participate in a ceremony to honor and recognize the work they have done dealing with their key issues.

POSSIBILITIES

We have experienced many and different "ceremonies" due to the interests of each person. We provide some information that gives them a framework to build their own expression of closure. The important message we give is of respect for that person's decision. It is especially important to remember that by developing trust and communication, this person is now ready to take a "giant leap of faith" (in themselves) and be in a risky situation.

We've had letters written forgiving family members who haven't been supportive. Once, the letters were attached to two separate helium balloons. They were released and the person waved good-bye with a beaming smile. People have chosen to write poetry to express the transitions experience. Others have used the symbol of a butterfly to identify what has changed.

Another person chose to light a candle and focus on what she was still going to work on and how she has learned to cope with it. A candle for the future—looking ahead with hope.

And of course we end each "graduation" with food and drink for all. Lots of congratulations from everyone and expectations go with the future graduate.

CONTRIBUTOR

Diane Groff
819 Sumner Street
Longmont, CO 80501, USA
(303) 772-2351

VERTIGO—THE BALANCE BROOM AS A METAPHOR FOR THE NATURAL IMBALANCE OF LIFE

INTRODUCTION

The activity involved with this metaphor has traditionally been called the Balance Broom. I call this activity Vertigo. It was originally designed as an ice-breaker to establish an environment within a group, where it is okay to look foolish in front of other people, thereby reducing the inhibitions of the group.

A person inside a circle of people spins around 10–15 times with his or her head resting against the top of a bat or blunt stick, which is about waist- high. The challenge is to drop the blunt stick or bat on the ground and then attempt to step over it.

Metaphorically, spinning is ment to represent the imbalance in life that naturally occurs with change. Stepping over the (vertigo) stick metaphorically represents a "rite of passage."

I first tried this application of the activity with a class of fifth-graders during their last physical education class of the year. They were leaving elementary school and moving on to middle school. I have also used this activity at the end of a 14-day Outward Bound course with 12–13-year-old males. These applications of the activity were designed to process an experience of a group during the separation or termination stage of development. The application of this metaphor to different groups is dependent only upon the creativity of its facilitator.

SET-UP

The set-up for this activity is a circle where everyone is able to see each other. The facilitator describes the continuum of choices that the participants can use to challenge and express themselves. Once the activity is clearly understood, then the facilitator places the stick in the center and waits for a volunteer to enter the circle. I have found that going first as an instructor sets the tone for the risk-taking involved in the activity.

SAMPLE PRESENTATION

"Before presenting this activity, I would like to share a reading with you so that you can think about its message while you are doing this activity.

'Balancing is a feeling of being in touch with one's body, of continually centering energy with the cooperation and conscious support of all other body parts. So, we are in the constant process of changing. Change always carries with it a period of imbalance: the scariness and excitement of new possibilities. This happens when something new is being added or something old is going. The feeling of imbalance is often one of confusion. The picture of imbalance can be one of physical illness (anger and fear) . . . Any imbalance is a message about some change taking place. This is a perfectly natural phase because while we are in the process of rebalancing imbalance has to take place first.'[1]

Life is a constant process of sorting through the many parts of yourself that contribute to your identity. There may be parts about yourself that you may decide to leave behind, change, or keep. This 'sorting of parts' may cause imbalance during times of change along your lifeline. This imbalance is natural. It is part of life. It's a message that is telling you that change is taking place.

The name of this activity is Vertigo. Vertigo is the sensation you feel when you're on a merry-go-round or a wild rotating amusement park ride. You feel like your body is rotating around in circles. It's also similar to the way you may feel when you're changing. You feel different, out of balance.

The challenge of Vertigo is to spin your body around the 'Vertigo stick' while keeping your head on the top of it. Then, you drop the stick on the ground and attempt to step over it. You may choose the speed at which you spin and how many times you turn around. For example, if you are uncomfortable with spinning, then you may hold the stick in your hand, walk and pivot around in a circle while making eye contact with each member in the group. Or, you can spin around 10 times as fast as you can and then attempt to step over the stick. You decide what you want to do (a demonstration along with these examples will help the participants understand the activity). Remember to place your head gently on the stick before you start to spin.

---

1. From *Peoplemaking* by V. Satir, 1972, Palo Alto, CA: Science and Behavior Books.

After you spin around and step over the stick, I would like you to name a part of yourself that you value and want to take with you into the future. What quality, attribute, or part of yourself are you going to take with you when you enter middle school? What will help you with this next period of your life? Take some time to think about what part you want take with you. When you are ready, then you may enter the circle and use the Vertigo stick." (Again, this could be a good time for the facilitator to set the tone by going first.)

If the individual has difficulty thinking of a quality or part, then the group can assist the individual in thinking of one. Allow the group time to think about what part they want to take with them and allow them to enter the middle of the circle when they are ready. You could also reemphasize "challenge by choice" at this point.

SAFETY CONSIDERATIONS

1. Appropriate spotting techniques such as supporting the head of the person.
2. The surface area of the activity should be relatively forgiving.
3. If a stick is used, then it should be blunt, and/or the top surface should be padded. Potential impalements should also be identified (e.g., eye).
4. Hands should be overlapping and crossed while placed on top of the stick.

DEBRIEFING

Most of the time I have found that the processing of this experience occurs during the activity. The framing of the activity and quote seem quite powerful, and little, if any, further discussion is necessary.

CONTRIBUTOR

Bob Davis (a.k.a. Bobby D.)
Graduate Student
Department of Kinesiology
New Hampshire Hall
124 Main Street
Durham, NH 03825-3559, USA

UTILIZATION THEORY: DESIRE FOR CHANGE AND THE WALL

INTRODUCTION

This introduction has been used successfully with a number of initiatives (e.g., Trust Fall, Pamper Pole, Trust Lean, Rappelling the Wall). The frame can work almost anywhere in the therapeutic process. It works with a variety of client groups including psychiatric, chemically dependent, therapists, and adolescents.

GOAL

1. To help clients identify behaviors that no longer work for them.
2. To identify more useful behaviors.
3. To have clients experience themselves utilizing these more useful behaviors.

SET-UP

For this discussion I utilize this introduction as it pertains to the Wall (please remember it can be used for numerous activities). Generally I suggest introducing the safety aspects of the activity prior to doing this introduction. If possible or practical, the identification of "old behaviors and new behaviors" can happen prior to engaging in the activity. This might be in the form of a group discussion, journal activity, or similar process where the clients have explored the concept of behaviors that don't work for them.

SAMPLE PRESENTATION

"I want you to look at this wall and think of a behavior, a way of acting, or a way of thinking that is blocking you from doing what you want to do or from being the person you want to be. How does it block you; how does it get in your way? I want you to think of a behavior that is concrete and specific and that is manageable in size. Before you share your thoughts, I'm going to ask you to think about how you would change this behavior so that it wouldn't block you. How would you get over this behavior? (Pause added here.) If you're ready, let's share both the behavior that stops you and how you would like to change it." (Note: You may need to work with some of the participants to get them to be concrete and specific.)

"We know that it is very hard to make changes alone, just as it is difficult to go over this wall alone. This group is going to help each other make the changes you just talked about, just as you are going to help each other get over that old behavior. I'm going to ask you to leave behind the behavior that doesn't work for you any more. So before you go up over the wall, I want you to leave behind that old way of being." (Note: Use the clients' language as much as possible). "You may want to say something like 'I'm leaving my behavior down here.' As you begin to leave behind that old behavior I want you to say, 'I'm moving up.' If this is clear, you will have 45 minutes for the activity." (Note: Do not hesitate to stop the process, especially if you see people moving back to old behavior. Utilize what the client is saying and doing.)

CONSIDERATIONS

Language can be a powerful tool, as can the natural metaphors inherent in the activity. For example, many of the trust activities (Trust Fall, Rappel, Pamper Pole) have a natural "letting go" component. Many have utilized this letting go with the Trust Fall, but fewer with other activities. Some clients will respond better to words like "letting go," others to "leaving behind." Pay attention to what your group members say. The Pamper Pole has an element of going out and getting something that is not present in the other activities mentioned. If someone talks about just needing to do it to commit to the change, perhaps the Pamper Pole will be more isomorphic than the Trust Fall.

I have seen other ideas incorporated with this type of introduction. Have each person create a totem for the behavior they are leaving behind. Have them leave this totem behind. When they get to the new place have them chose another. This is particularly effective with a rappel, as the top of the site is usually different than the bottom. Have the individuals shout out what they are leaving behind and what they are replacing it with. Have them play out this old behavior or identify what we would see if they were doing this old behavior. Have others act out the person doing this old behavior. Have them identify what the new behavior would look like; have them act out the new behavior.

DEBRIEFING

Questions may include:

1. What allowed you to make the changes in your behavior that you wanted?
2. What kept you stuck or blocked from making those changes?
3. How did others help or hinder you making the changes you wanted?

Focus the process on linking the experience of going over the wall to that of changing their behavior. Help the clients to identify what they actually changed, and what might still be a "wall."

CONTRIBUTOR

Christian Itin, MSW
1350 Balsam Avenue
Boulder, CO 80304, USA
(303) 442-2189

TEAR DOWN THE WALL

INTRODUCTION

During the past few years I have tried to design initiative/activity sequences with multiple approaches to enhance the metaphor building process and increase the positive impact of an initiative. Clearly, metaphors that a facilitator draws from a client's world have a greater impact than metaphors prepared by facilitators on their own and then presented to the client. Tear Down the Wall is a sequenced activity that permits each participant to design their own metaphor for the wall initiative. Tear Down the Wall is a guided vision/imagery, creative art therapy, experiential therapy activity. It requires a three-hour minimum time commitment to complete.

GOALS

This activity is designed to facilitate participants' self-awareness and insight into:

1. Thoughts, feelings, and actions.
2. Quality world pictures.
3. Creative reorganization of coping behaviors.
4. Problem-solving skill development.

This activity permits participants to construct their own individual metaphors from their world. The meta-message of the entire sequence is that unsolvable "problems" are illusory; the real roadblocks to reorganization are within ourselves, and other resources often can help foster reorganization and bring "success." (For a detailed discussion of quality world and reorganization process, read *Control Theory* by William Glasser.)

PREPARATION/SET-UP

Materials needed for this activity include:

1. Access to a comfortable space where participants can lie down, relax, and close their eyes (an inside space with pillows works quite well).
2. Art supplies (including construction paper, newsprint, crayons, paints, pens, pencils).
3. Access to a wall initiative.

DESCRIPTION

Visualization (30–40 minutes)

The facilitator, through guided imagery and metaphor, assists participants in identifying thoughts, feelings, and actions that historically, currently, and potentially hinder participants from getting what they really want.

An effective framework is to ask participants to lie down, get comfortable, and close their eyes. Ask them to focus on their breathing and in a soothing voice encourage them to be relaxed and focused. Any familiar scenario to explore barriers that prevent participants from meeting the quality world pictures they hold is effective.

It is important to note that participants sometimes fall asleep, depending on the breadth and depth of the facilitator's focus on relaxation and breathing techniques. This is okay, and participants will respond more positively if they know this.

After the visualization exercise is complete, the facilitator asks participants to share for a brief moment what the experience was like. There is no need to debrief learnings and insights at this point; those learnings will be expressed in the next activity.

Creative Art Activity (30–45 minutes)

Following the visualization, participants are asked to design individual "bricks" using paper, scissors, markers, and paints. Participants are asked to evaluate various aspects of the behaviors identified in the visualization and express these in the size, color, and drawings on each brick.

Key concepts to bring up include: (1) color as a means to express thoughts, feelings, and actions, (2) brick size to express relative intensity, and (3) simple geometric shapes, squiggle lines, etc. as a means to express relationships and ideas. Artistic ability is not a prerequisite for this activity, and participants who are aware of this will have an easier time expressing themselves.

Group Discussion (45–60 minutes)

Following this expressive activity, a facilitator conducts a process group during which each participant places their bricks on a blank wall and explains their significance. Through discussion and consultation with the group, each participant has an opportunity to creatively reorganize these behaviors. Upon completion, a "wall" should be apparent from the placement of the individual "bricks."

Note: There is an opportunity at this point to explore if any individuals can break through their wall without the help of others.

The Wall Initiative (30–45 minutes)

Following the group discussion, participants are given the opportunity to address the wall initiative following standard guidelines and site-specific rules. After completion of this initiative, the activity sequence as an entirety is briefly processed.

Note: The investment of participants in the wall is very high by this point. The facilitator can provide a significant intervention with any participants who, during the group discussion, claimed an ability to break through their "wall" without the help of others by providing them with an opportunity to complete the wall initiative under the same guidelines as the group.

DEBRIEFING

The context of this activity sequence is framed with an overall metaphor that people build walls for a purpose, but barriers that keep others out keep us in. Additional metaphors can be developed from participants' "world pictures."

Debriefing for this activity should be ongoing throughout the sequence so that the final discussion following completion of the wall initiative is concise and poignant.

Areas to emphasize during the discussions include:

1. People choose their feelings, thoughts, and actions; all are aspects of behavior and directed toward controlling our environment.

2. All behavior is purposeful.
3. Reorganization has its foundation in individual imagination and creativity.

CONTRIBUTOR

G. Scott Graham
Thompson Island Outward Bound
Education Center
Boston, MA 02127, USA
(617) 328-3900

CREATING "PERSONAPHORS" THROUGH PERSONAL DISCLOSURE ACTIVITIES

INTRODUCTION

Structured, personal disclosure activities can help create a safe environment for group members to take the risks associated with expressing thoughts, feelings, beliefs, self-concepts, and life experiences. Personal disclosure activities can also be a catalyst to help people communicate metaphorically. Connections are often developed between affect and insight through concrete and visual metaphors, since a large degree of learning can result from bodily experienced sensations (Singer, 1973). People experience their bodies and learnings through right brain processes associated with sensory perceptions. Mills and Crowley (1986) indicate that metaphors are the language of the right brain where processing experiences is imagistic (visual), emotional (feelings), and kinesthetic (physical tasks). Each person has a preferred sensory mode of absorbing, assimilating, and recalling information (Dolan, 1986).

The personal disclosure activities described below can help create a safer environment for people to develop their personal metaphors and establish a foundation to trust others. As a result, group members begin to share of themselves intimately. Smith (1993) infers that alternative personal disclosure activities:

> . . . *facilitate an atmosphere of trust and honest communication, where group members find acceptance and understanding sufficient to reveal true feelings, fears, and conflicts. The sharing of these emotions and revelations, with the acceptance/support of the group at hand, leads to personal growth and learning (p. 285).*

Refer to Wybenga and Spagnuolo (1991) concerning the structure of warm-up activities and Smith (1993) for alternative methodologies for processing group and individual/group experiences. The following are a sample of personal disclosure activities that have worked well for me.

"TOYS-R-US"

Collect 50 or more small toys and objects (e.g., wooden blocks, army men, plastic animals). Spread these items on the floor in the middle of the group. Instruct participants to look at and touch the objects to become familiar with the collection. After about two minutes, the facilitator asks each participant to pick out two objects, one that represents how they see themselves and one to depict how others might see them. Proceed around the circle with each member individually showing their objects to the group with an explanation of their symbolic meaning. A less abstract instruction would be to ask the participants to select toys that remind them of an event in their life or a representation of something of personal meaning. Adolescents have become more engaged with this personal disclosure activity by selecting an object that reminds them of another member of the group. Having each member who discloses their "Toys-R-Us" story select the next person they want to hear from has stimulated a deeper level of participation and engagement, rather than a sequential whip or open volunteering (adapted from Wybenga & Spagnuolo, 1991).

TOUCHY-FEELY

Collect objects and materials that have specific tactile significance (fabrics, sandpaper, sponges, hand cream, etc.). Spread these items on the floor in the middle of the group. Instruct the participants to pick up the objects to feel the various textures. After about two minutes, the facilitator asks each member to select two or more objects, one that represents their feeling about themselves (real self) and one that represents how they feel they portray themselves to others (public self). This activity will be helpful to people that primarily communicate and experience life kinesthetically (feeling, touch) (inspired by Kitty Hunt-Johnson).

WISH YOU WERE HERE

Collect black-and-white photographic postcards that depict people engaged in various aspects of daily life. Spread the postcards on the floor in the middle of the group and instruct the group to look at the various images. After about two minutes, ask the group to select several postcards that have some personal meaning (event from childhood, a positive experience, a desired experience, or whatever feels appropriate). Extensions of this activity that could access the visual sensory system are photographic postcard collections of various animals, aquatic scenes and land forms, automobiles and modes of transportation, weather patterns, and trees and flowers (adapted from Wybenga and Spagnuolo, 1991).

COLOR MY WORLD

Go to your neighborhood paint supply store and ask for a collection of color swatches. Spread the rainbow of color swatches on the floor in the middle of the group. After several minutes, ask the members to pick a color swatch that represents how they feel or see themselves. Ask each person to articulate the personal meaning the color symbolizes for them. Does the color selected represent the person's real self or public self? The personal metaphor created could represent how each member feels at that moment or how they generally see themselves in the world.

GOOFY

Pick up a finger puppet of the Disney character Goofy. Explain to the group that each of us makes mistakes in daily living and sometimes we act in ways that are embarrassing to mention to other people. Goofing up is normal and we all have goofed up in similar ways. One purpose of this personal disclosure activity is to help each of us realize that we are not alone in our mistakes. Another goal is to enhance learning from these mistakes. The facilitator closes his/her eyes as Goofy is passed around the circle and says to stop after a few seconds. The person with Goofy relays a story of a time when they goofed up, followed by the remainder of the group raising their hands if they have a similar story. The storyteller closes their eyes as Goofy is passed person to person around the circle and says "stop" after a few seconds. The person with Goofy tells their embarrassing story and the game proceeds. Extensions of this activity design could be using a finger puppet of Pinnochio in which the participants tell stories of times they regret not telling the truth. Another extension could be passing around a plastic fish and telling about situations or feeling like a "fish out of water" in a group (adapted from Jude, Leadership Decisions Institute, Camp Kieve).

UNGAME FISHBOWL

Purchase a version of the Ungame question cards (Teen, Kids, Couples, Families, and All Ages, marketed by Talicor Incorporated, Anaheim, CA). Put the question cards in a fishbowl or hat. Pass them around the group with each person reaching in the bowl to grab three cards. Then have each member pick one question to answer themselves and select someone else in the group to answer the other. The remaining card allows the participants choice as to which cards to answer. Turns proceed around the circle. Remember to be flexible and design this activity in any manner you or the group desires. An extension could involve the participants writing their own question cards. This activity leads into a discussion of listening skills, following up on new insights into another person after the group session, and feedback skills (adapted from Wybenga and Spagnuolo, 1991).

SPLIT IMAGES

Take a black-and-white photograph of each participant. The picture must be taken with the subject looking straight into the camera as if posing for a driver's license photograph. Ask the photographic store to make one normal print and another in which the negative is flipped upside down. Cut the two photographs precisely through the middle of the face (between the eyes through the middle of the nose). Tape the two left sides together to make one complete facial image and tape the two right sides together. Ask the participants to study the photographs to comment on the different expressions and feelings they notice from the right to left side composite photographs of each person.

ADDITIONAL PERSONAL DISCLOSURE METHODS

1. Design a personal traits search (Bingo) based on information from student files.
2. Use the Feelings Marketplace cards marketed through Project Adventure.
3. Describe a recent horrible day and a recent terrific day.
4. Describe one positive and one negative thing about _____.
5. Describe the characteristics of someone you admire.
5. Describe your current state of being based on a weather report.

CONTRIBUTOR

Andy Greif
RR 1, Box 3082
Kennebunk, ME 04043, USA
(207) 985-3727

CLIMBING OUT OF SHAME

INTRODUCTION

This exercise is designed to bring into awareness the personal dynamics of shame. The participants may know how horrible it feels to experience shame, yet most of us are very unaware of the actual psychological and physiological reactions we have to feeling shame. True recovery from any trauma, abuse, addiction, or disorder often requires people to learn about and reclaim the part of themselves that not only feels shameful but reacts to it in a personally destructive way. The way to begin the process of reclaiming the self is to slow down the shame spiral enough to become aware of specific personal triggers and the chain of reactions that lead to a state of feeling resourceless and of having low self-esteem. This state of resourcelessness and low self-esteem may become so great that the person may experience a shame blackout, inability to track, tunnel vision, inability to communicate, etc. The internal tension and pain can also be so great at this point that the person seeks addictive or compulsive behaviors to numb this internal pain. These behaviors might include chemical use, sex, working too much, watching too much TV, eating disorders, rage, etc. The process of personal response to shame may be unconscious (i.e., completely out of conscious awareness of the individual involved in the throes of the shame spiral).

GOALS

1. Increase awareness of personal shame triggers.
2. Increase awareness of personal physiological reaction to shame.
3. Recognition of the addictive urge when shame has been triggered.
4. To begin the process of reclaiming the self and the shaking off of shame.

SET-UP

General Activity: Climbing Wall or Rock Climbing.

Material: All standard climbing equipment plus paper, clipboards (or sturdy flat surface to write on), and pens. Blindfolds may be used for those participants who are particularly adept at climbing or feel very resourceful while climbing. These people may be blindfolded while they climb as a way to slow them down enough to become aware of and acknowledge their feelings and physical response to shame statements.

Contraindications: This exercise is only appropriate after the participants have become familiar with climbing and belaying and have had at least one successful climb. They need to know they can do the climb both psychologically and physiologically before we introduce shame. They need to be somewhat aware of their process of self-discovery, and though participants enter treatment at different levels of personal awareness, they should possess at least two weeks into treatment before using this tool. This tool may require a more advanced level of personal awareness than some persons with certain psychiatric diagnoses may possess at this point in treatment. Because we are dealing with the power of a full-blown body reaction to personalized shame, the facilitator must work in an extremely gentle, responsive, and compassionate manner.

SAMPLE PRESENTATION

"You hear a lot about shame when you're in treatment. And you get the sense, especially those of you that are in or through with family week, that shame is one of the emotions that are behind or underlying your disease. So first let's talk a little about shame. What is shame? How is shame different from guilt?" (Start a dialogue brainstorming different ideas on shame and guilt.) "So, basically guilt is when you think you did something, a behavior that is wrong or bad, and shame is when you think you are wrong or bad. Do you see the difference? One is about the behavior or action and the other is about you. You are not good enough, not worthy enough, you are "less than;" you are broken, bad, wrong, or worthless. How many of you have felt this way before?

We pick up these messages from the people around us. Our parents, relatives, teachers, friends, lovers, co-workers, supervisors, etc. And the interesting thing about shame is that you only pass on the shame if you have been shamed yourself. A shame-based system perpetuates or, more accurately, perpetrates shame. The more shamed you are, the more you will pass on shame. And sometimes for some of us, the shame can be so great inside ourselves that we hit a shame spiral. This is when the shame triggers a response in us and we recoil. And this spiral continues downward until something interferes with it, breaks the pattern, and we start feeling better and more grounded, more real about ourselves, *or* we hit a shame blackout.

A shame blackout happens when you feel more shame than you are capable of handling at that moment. Some people actually experience tunnel vision where their peripheral vision becomes darkened and they can only see what is directly in front of them. Hearing may become impaired as the person may only be hearing the old shaming messages inside them.

When we experience and get triggered by shame, one of the most common reactions is to leave our body, to check out for awhile and let our mind float around somewhere else. When we leave our bodies, we lose strength. As we become aware of this happening today when we climb, we will actually be able to tell at what moment the strength leaves and we start checking out. When we do this out in the world (and in our families), we do it as a survival mechanism and it works. The only thing is that being around shame and being in a survival mode, whether it's in the situation we are in or the shame we carry around inside us, can be very painful, stressful, and create a lot of tension within us. At some point the tension and pain may trigger us into a disease behavior as a way to try and find some sort of relief.

So, in recovery, as we become aware of our disease and what triggers it, we become aware of the underlying emotions and what we do when emotions are triggered that we are uncomfortable with, such as shame.

To begin this exercise, you need to get into pairs. Each of you take a piece of paper and draw a line down the middle, creating two columns. For the heading at the top of one column write Men and the other column will be Women. Now write down all the shame messages men have given to you in that column. That might include your father, male relatives, boys at school, men co-workers, romantic partner, etc. In the Female column put all the shame messages that women have given to you. Ask each other questions about this to help remember what these messages were. Examples may be 'I didn't think you were that dumb' or 'You're crazy, you could never do that' (allow plenty of time for the participants to complete this part, go around and assist them to uncover past and current shame statements, gestures, images, etc.).

Now, team up with another pair and decide who is going to climb first and who is going to belay. The climber will give their paper to the other two people who will stand with the belayer and say these shame statements to you with conviction while you are climbing. Those of you saying the shame statements may start to improvise what you are saying to fit the situation of the climber once you get a sense for what sort of shame statements they have. The climber's goal is not necessarily to climb to the top, but to recognize how their body reacts to shame and what their body does when it gets triggered by shame."

Instructor/therapists at this point walk around to the various groups climbing and chime in, shouting shame statements to the climbers as they climb. If you have a particularly strong climber who appears to be unaffected by their own shame statements, then you probably have someone who is trying to "out climb" their shame. Many of these people may use exercise as a way to avoid, and exercise can become very compulsive for them. Blindfolding these people to slow them down and get them more present with this exercise may help.

After a climber has climbed once, and has experienced their shame response (you will be able to see this in their "minimal cues" such as skin coloring, body posture, eye contact, etc.), have them come down and shake out the shame. Demonstrate for them how to shake their arms and legs out and shout, yell, scream to get the shame out. For most people, this will take several times for them to shake out all the shame and get themselves grounded again. You will also be able to tell when they are present and grounded again by their "minimal cues."

"Now I want the climbers to climb again. When they hear their shame statements, they should reply with a personally affirming statement. This could be a confrontation such as 'When you (behavior), I feel (emotion), like when you say shaming things to me I feel sad and angry.' Or, the climbers could say an affirmation to the shaming statements such as 'I am learning from all my experiences in a growthful way.' In other words, the climbers want to reply to the shame statements in a way that assists and affirms themselves. Again, the climbers want to pay attention to how their body responds to hearing and feeling resourceful and personally affirming statements and messages as replies in the face of shame."

Some people may do very well with this part and their sense of humor and playfulness may come out. This is to be encouraged. Some people may take several tries at climbing, coming down and shaking off the shame, and climbing again before they start to free themselves from the trigger of shame. Some people may need to get angry to begin to empower themselves in the face of shame. This is to be encouraged, as often these are the people who never allow themselves to be rightfully angry.

SAFETY CONCERNS

Physical: All participants must be familiar with climbing and belaying before they do this exercise.

Staff needs to always keep an eye on the belayer and encourage them to break the climber off after every move, as they could fall at any time and often during this exercise.

Emotional: Whenever processes around shame are being done, especially experiential processes, extreme care must be taken. There is always the risk of someone being triggered by the shame into deeper abusive or traumatic memories. Because of this, staff needs to be as perceptive as possible, noticing everyone's cues and bringing them back into the present with comments and questions that lead the participants' awareness to what is happening now. The staffs' presence must be experienced by the participants as safe, gentle, compassionate, aware, and trustworthy. The experience of shame can create a deep sense of vulnerability and exposure. This dynamic must be respected and understood by the staff for the benefit to be gleaned from any experiential shame exercise.

DEBRIEFING

Sample Questions:

1. Did you experience shame while climbing?
2. How did you know you experienced shame?
3. What were the statements that really got to you?
4. Did any other memories come up when you experienced the shame?
5. Did you notice when the shame came into your body and the strength left?
6. Did you feel yourself start to leave your body?
7. What could you have done to try and stay in your body?
8. What were the things you used to do when you felt shame like that?

9. What was the cost to you of those reactionary behaviors? What effects did they have on your life?
10. How did it feel to climb to the shaming messages the second time and say your affirmations or confrontations reply?
11. Were you able to retain more strength doing this?
12. Were you able to stay in your body this time?
13. In what potentially shaming situations out in the world or in your families would you like to have more personal empowerment?
14. Having done this, what sort of resources would help you to deal with shaming situations in your life?
15. What sort of support do you need to start using those resources in your life?

CONTRIBUTOR

Daniel J. Meyers, Program Manager
Wilderness Recovery Program
Sierra Tucson Hospitals
16500 N. Lago Del Oro Parkway
Tucson, AZ 85737, USA
(800) 624-9001 ext. 2119

WINDOW OF TIME

GOAL

To be able to devise solutions to "problems" (setbacks) participants may face in the future.

LOGISTICS

Time required: 30–60 minutes.

Materials needed: A Spider's Web or a length of rope at least 10 feet long and some jingle bells. Tie the ropes between the backs of two chairs (chair backs approximately 3 feet apart) to form a vertical circle or window large enough for group members to pass through with some challenge. Jingle bells can be attached to the window (or Web) to sound out the "setbacks."

SET-UP

The object is to have each participant pass through the window (or web) without touching the rope or ringing the bells. Should the participant touch the rope or ring the bells, they return and start the activity over. Once a member is through, they cannot go back in order to help members who have yet to pass through the window. They can only help from their side.

If a "successful" participant chooses to help people remaining on the other side, they will have to begin again should there be physical contact with the person passing through the web or with the window. This means there is a consequence for helping—if the helped or helper has a "setback" (e.g., there is a risk in commitment to others).

SAMPLE PRESENTATION

Many times, the prediction of possible problems (setbacks) can allow for strategies to develop solutions to them before they happen and paradoxically prevent them from happening. The need for help in being successful in this activity can be related to asking others for help in achieving one's goals. I find this a very useful introduction to a Spider's

Web or adaptation of a Spider's Web for use indoors where minimal props/space are needed. In fact, it can easily be done with a couple or family size "group."

I tell the group in my set-up that the window represents a way to move from where they are now (the present) to where they wish to be (the future). The bells and the rope can represent setbacks the participant may encounter along the way.

DEBRIEFING

The setbacks encountered in the activity can be named by each participant (prior to or after the experience) and the group can brainstorm ways in which these actual setbacks might be prevented.

The price of helping others (commitment) can be examined in the participant's choice to help someone through, and perhaps have to return and complete the activity again should that person be faced with a setback. What are the real-life costs of helping others? What are real-life issues where a setback can occur from helping?

The relationship of being helped from the "future" side can be related to those who have "made it" wanting to help those "less fortunate" whether it is perceived to be needed or not. How/when can "helpers" be useful? Harmful? In what specific areas would the participant like help? When? When not?

CONTRIBUTOR

H. L. "Lee" Gillis
Georgia College
Psychology Department
Milledgeville, GA 31061, USA
(912) 454-0865
and
Project Adventure, Inc.
Covington, GA

LIFE'S A RIVER

INTRODUCTION

This metaphor is applicable to people who have white water paddling experience, or may be used along with a white water kayaking class. Ideally, it would be used within the framework of a 10-day residential program aimed at developing white water kayaking skills, life-skills, and self-esteem. I have found this metaphor to be particularly useful in understanding my own healing. It could really intergrate nicely with an adventuresome, established, incest survivor group.

The metaphor is essentially that life has many parallels to kayaking a river. There are "rapids" ranging from Class I to Class VI that pop up every day. Every rapid poses its own set of hazards and rewards. Boaters flip over and usually roll up; sometimes they swim. Fear is common while kayaking—it's how the boater identifies and works with it that makes the difference. Along with increasing skill comes the knowledge that, even after a flip, a roll can happen.

Even a boater with good rolling and bracing skills has an occasional mishap and ends up in the river. That boater needs to know swimming skills to stay as safe as possible while in the river. Many safety precautions are involved in a river trip. Before the trip, the boater checks all gear for damage, and a helmet and lifejacket are always worn. Once on the river, boaters run safety for each other, setting up in and below rapids to provide immediate assistance in the event of a swim.

GOALS

1. Develop and understand the importance of a support network.
2. Learn to take proper precautions for personal safety.
3. Learn to set healthy, safe boundaries.

EXPERIENCE LEVEL

A white water kayaking program designed to take participants from beginner to competent Class II–III boaters within 10 days is required.

SUCCESSFUL RESOLUTION

1. Group and individual members giving and receiving support.
2. Individual members looking after their own safety needs.
3. Individuals setting and sticking to personal boundaries.

FRAMEWORK

1. Provide instructions in language transferable to other issues.
2. Stress importance of safety systems and the interdependence of group safety.
3. Allow participants to be responsible for their own safety and equipment.
4. Stress the choice to portage or run larger rapids. Support that choice.
5. Teach good "bracing" techniques in addition to "rolling."
6. Draw parallels as white water skill and awareness grow.

MOTIVATION

1. Sequence activities in a reasonable progression of skill.
2. Be attentive to group development.
3. Ensure participants are comfortable with new skills.
4. Review connections between new river skills and objectives to ensure isomorphic connections.

REVISE IN PROCESS

1. Maintain safety—make adjustments where appropriate.
2. Provide appropriate reframing.

DEBRIEF

1. Use debriefs to emphasize isomorphic connections.
2. Focus debrief discussion around goals.

SAMPLE PRESENTATION

"This morning's activity will be learning to side surf your kayak. Side surfing a kayak can be very similar to taking on disturbing issues during therapy or having emotions triggered by a surprise event. At first it may be scary and disorienting and you will feel out of control. The skills you learn as you practice today can be like learning in therapy. Honing these skills in a safe environment, with the support and safety of the group, may help you if you find your emotions triggered by an unexpected event.

On the river, we will proceed to a hole where we can learn and practice side surfing. You can enter this particular hole by choice. Experiment with your 'bracing' and 'rolling' skills. The more you practice, the more comfort and control you will have. Other members of the group will be available to help you rescue yourself if you need to swim. At first, some boaters will be more daring while others hang back in the eddy. Remember to bring your helmet and lifejacket to keep you safe while you're out there.

It is your choice to try side surfing. You may choose not to. I recommend it as a worthwhile skill to protect you when you venture into the larger rapids where you may wander into a large hole by surprise. You can count on the group for assistance if you run into problems. You may also want to discuss what does and doesn't work among yourselves and with your instructors.

Remember to relax and focus. You may find that acknowledging your fear will actually positively affect your ability. Don't forget your safety equipment and remember the group when you need help."

RIVER RUNNING

"This afternoon we will be headed out on the river for an afternoon of paddling. Similar to your life and your healing, you may be running several rapids that vary in difficulty. Some rapids, like your life experiences, may be easy with few hazards and easy-to-find routes. Other rapids may have difficult routes with many hazards. There will be rocks to avoid, waves that might catch you by surprise, and holes that may stop you and even surf you for a while.

Like this morning, you will need to use good coping skills like bracing and rolling to finish the day without swimming. The more you integrate these skills into your repertoire, the less you find yourself swimming. Unlike the morning you will find that, like life, the group will not be as readily available for assistance. You need to remember what it will take to keep you safe: your life jacket, helmet, and your good judgment. Listen to your intuition, that little voice that may tell you to carry a rapid. Maybe you've heard this voice before, telling you to avoid a particular person or situation and you may not have had the choice to listen and act on it. Like this morning, you need to pay attention to your fear. You may have felt similar fear at other times in your life and not known what to do about it. Feel free to discuss your fear with the group as we go along. You can talk in eddies, on stretches of flatwater, or while we are out of the boats for breaks and scouting.

If you find yourself swimming, take steps to keep yourself safe. Do the simple things: Breathe when you can; don't when you can't. You may have tunnel vision—only being able to see the waves right in front of your face. You may feel outright panic, but it will end quickly and the group will be there to help you. Remember, you always come out at the bottom. Perhaps worse for the wear, but you always come out. The river is always moving downstream.

When we encounter the more significant rapids, we will set up organized safety to take care of each other. There will be boaters on shore with ropes, and paddlers in boats at the end to help you get back together should you swim. The group will be more available for support should you need it. There are times when you may find yourself in the support role. Remember to keep yourself safe, then do what you can for the other person.

We will scout each rapid from shore and you may learn to pick out the hazards. Should you find yourself in a hole, remember the coping skills you learned to help you survive. Throughout your life you've learned to brace very well, but remember also that you have a fairly reliable roll, and if you do tip over you will probably right yourself. When you come upright, find an eddy where you can stop and collect your thoughts, relax, and rest. Again, the group will be there for you if the situation becomes too much.

Most importantly, enjoy yourself. Work the river and the boat. It will feel great and you may even have fun too!"

CONTRIBUTOR

Steph Barrett
Unity College
Box 518
Unity, ME 04988, USA
(207) 948-3125

STANDING EGG

INTRODUCTION

The main purpose of this activity is to facilitate problem-solving and group interaction. This activity has been used in a short-term crisis intervention psychiatric program as a warm-up exercise in the Solution Focus Group.

GOAL

This activity can be an effective way to engage individuals to look at alternative ways to solve problems and take new risks. It is also a way to increase social interaction and provides an opportunity for individuals to utilize each other in the problem-solving process.

SET-UP

All that is needed is one raw egg and a room with a hard floor surface.

SAMPLE PRESENTATION

"We are going to begin with an experiential exercise to assist you in looking at different solutions to a problem. We would like the group to work together in coming up with the solution.

This is a raw egg and your task is to stand this egg in an upright position on the hard surface. Nothing can be touching the egg to support it in the upright position."

LOGISTICS

Allow the group to work on this problem for up to 10 minutes and then process the individuals' feelings around this problem-solving task.

One solution to the initiative is that the group gently taps the egg on a hard surface until the bottom of the egg shell breaks enough to hold the egg in an upright position.

DEBRIEFING

The group does not have to come up with a solution for processing to be useful. Here are some examples of questions and statements that may be useful in processing this activity: "How does it feel to be stuck? How does it feel to take a risk? Sometimes the obvious solution is the correct answer. How does it feel to be successful? How does it feel to get support? How does it feel not to get any support? Can you see how your method of problem-solving continues to keep you stuck in your problem rather than looking at new solutions?"

CONTRIBUTOR

Paula Bartel, OTR
Schelly Trojan, CTRS
St. Joseph PsychCenter, 9th Floor
1650 Fillmore
Denver, CO 80206, USA

CORPORATE POPULATIONS

THE MEUSE AS A METAPHOR FOR BUSINESS OPERATIONS IN A CHANGING ENVIRONMENT

INTRODUCTION

The framing for this initiative has been used with a number of business organizations that are trying to manage their operations in response to numerous external changes. Some of these changes are environmental pressures placed upon their industry. Other changes are from quality competition that has recently taken market shares away from the client organization. The activity is best used as a way to help members of the organization demonstrate to themselves the importance of continuous improvement and to guard against their own complacency.

GOALS

Presented in the following manner, this initiative helps team members to emphasize: (1) the importance of diversity and the possibility of utilizing more than one approach to attain the desired results, (2) a healthy attitude toward critiquing one's own work to identify ways in which it might be improved, and (3) the utility of an established forum to implement "20th Century Technology" known as dialogue for process improvement and enhanced quality. This initiative, the Time Warp, can only be solved by dealing with these three issues. It therefore presents positive models of interaction for team members that can be applied to their jobs on a daily basis.

SET-UP

The basic set-up for the Time Warp is very similar to The Meuse as outlined in *Cowstails and Cobras II,* (Rohnke, 1989, p.87). The placement of the cinder blocks is critical to the effectiveness of this initiative problem. The significant difference is that the cinder blocks are placed closer together at the "starting" side of the swamp and gradually farther apart as the group progresses to the "finishing" side.

It is best to place these in such a way that the spacing differential is not visibly obvious to members before experimentation begins.

In the beginning, the group should be able to place a board at an angle and successfully bridge a gap. As they near the middle of the swamp this technique will no longer work, thanks to the cinder block placement (meant to mirror competition, change in the work place). The blocks in the middle of the swamp should be placed so as to not allow for the previously successful "angle" placement of boards. It works well to have the center of the swamp area set up just as in *Cowstails* where the placement of two boards into a "T" shape will provide a stable basis for foot placement and advancement. Continuing to the far side, the group will soon find that neither the "angle" nor the "T" placement is successful. At this point, they must come up with still another possibility of how to successfully accomplish the task. Cinder blocks on this "finishing" side should be carefully placed so that the "angle" and "T" methods must be altered, combined, metamorphosed, etc. to come up with a new solution. Usually the group will choose to place the nearest board (the one most underfoot) in such a way that a foot or so of it extends past a block and is used as a fulcrum or lever for the next board.

Obviously, spotting becomes more critical as the initiative advances in both time and complexity, so be prepared to emphasize safety concerns with the group. There comes a greater possibility that the groups will try more unconventional solutions, thus increasing the need for awareness of safety precautions by participants and instructors.

SAMPLE PRESENTATION

Participants are asked to stand in a circle and discuss for a few minutes the biggest obstacles they have encountered in their business lives over the past "X" years. If the discussion does not go in this direction on its own accord, attempt to steer the conversation toward describing the decade of the 60's in their industry, then the 70's, and so on. At the rate things are changing now, the participants may wish to address shorter, more recent periods of time. Questions may include "What types of challenges have you seen consistently through the years?" and "What are the constants of change?" A discussion of positive attitudes and behaviors to see the group through these challenges is facilitated.

Following this discussion, the set-up for the Time Warp takes place. Once the group is gathered on the starting side of the "swamp," the instructor then makes the analogy of how this is similar to starting up or continuing to operate a successful business venture during changing times.

"Along the way you may encounter safe places or islands of serenity where things are moving along fine, where you may find some stability. At other times, it may seem as though there is no plausible solution to the situation at hand. Things may seem to be wavering and unsure. Your goal is to use the limited resources, which a company may have available in a sluggish economy, to create a stable pathway through the changing times and into a successful and profitable future (the other side). Please keep in mind the things which you discussed earlier that you felt were positive behaviors or attitudes to get through such trying times."

The group is then given instructions as to what resources it has and what the parameters of the business environment have become. Be sure that these are as similar as possible to the home environment of the client in order to provide the proper isomorphic framing. Remember, we want them to say, "This is just like it is at work." This will provide a greater enhancement of learning and will enhance transfer to the work environment upon their return.

LOGISTICS

As a facilitator, I choose to step out of the process as much as possible, allowing the group to create its own learning. If the activity has been properly set up, intervention is necessary for safety reasons only. If asked to repeat the rules, I reflect back to them that they have all the tools and information they need to effectively solve the problem.

DEBRIEFING

If framed well, debriefing should flow easily out of completion of the activity. Discussion will begin to focus on behaviors and attitudes that helped the group to keep the business alive and growing. After exploring how things worked in this activity, facilitate this learning to how it is applicable to the work environment. Keep the goals of the activity in mind in guiding the session and you will find that the group will place considerable emphasis on the work environment themselves.

I prefer to spend most of the time debriefing this activity by having the group deal with the possible applications of the behaviors that enhance quality and deal effectively with change. Our clients have found this to be appropriate as well.

CONTRIBUTOR

Michael A. Lair, BA Industrial Psychology
Director, Venture Out!
Joy Outdoor Education Center
P.O. Box 157
Clarksville, OH 45113, USA
(513) 289-2031

THE SPIDER: A MEASURE OF QUALITY

INTRODUCTION

The following is an adaptation of the Spider's Web (Rohnke, 1989). It works well for groups working on Continuous Improvement or Total Quality Management (TQM) processes.

Use an isomorph that has you, the facilitator, as the group's customer. In this example, the group is working toward delivering "products" (people) to you through the web. As usual with this initiative, there are consequences for touches of the web. At an appropriate moment, such as when the group appears to be struggling with the quality of their approach to the activity, a "spider" can be balanced on one of the strands of the web. The spider would dangle precariously so that any vibration, due to a connection with the web, will knock it off. The spider therefore becomes a measure of the "quality" of the group's performance. The theme of this adaptation of the web initiative relates to determining and measuring quality in an organization. It works well for a particularly challenging web where the sizes of the holes are not too generous and touches of the web occur frequently.

GOAL

This initiative adaptation encourages participants to:

1. Partner with the customer to set criteria for determining quality.
2. Determine the consequences for a poor quality performance.
3. Develop processes for measuring quality in their organization.

SET-UP

Construct a spider, about four inches in diameter, from a durable material (i.e., plywood). Manufacture a small hook shape in one of the legs so that the spider balances on the web. Ensure that the spider falls off when the web is knocked.

SAMPLE PRESENTATION

During the presentation of the web initiative, encourage the group to partner with the customer (the facilitator) to determine what the consequences of a touch of the web will be during the activity. Ask the group to let the customer know when full delivery of the product (i.e., completion of the web) can be expected. This reinforces one of the central concepts of the quality movement: that quality revolves around the notion of the "customer." Quality is customer-driven in Total Quality Management. The customer's perspective is actively sought as a critical performance measure. In this manner, it is the customer who establishes the standards and expectations for quality and drives the process for continuous improvement.

Do not start by introducing the spider. Instead, allow the group to assess the quality of their performance. Watch to see how well they acknowledge touches of the web. Do they see all of the touches, so they are aware that there has been a quality problem? Are touches of the web consciously ignored? Do they expect the customer to recognize the quality glitches? The spider is best introduced when the group appears to be struggling with the management of their quality. Tell the group that their organization has developed a new "tool" for measuring quality in this process, and that the spider represents that tool. When the spider falls off the web, a quality error has occurred. The predetermined consequences then apply. In the TQM approach to doing business, the actual "tool" available for such measurement of processes is termed statistical process control (SPC). This is aimed at minimizing the special causes that lead to variation in the quality of a given process and at an overall improvement of the process.

DEBRIEFING

The activity challenges participants to explore the meaning of quality in their organization. In reality, there will always be some touches. How will the organization respond to these? How will they continue to improve? What role should the customer play in determining quality?

During the debrief, have the participants examine the difference in the quality of their performance before and after the introduction of the spider. What difference does the introduction of a measurement tool make to the overall quality of the performance? How can such tools be included to help assure quality in your organization?

The concrete examples of the web and the spider allow the philosophical discussion on quality to have relevance and meaning to all involved.

CONTRIBUTOR

Simon Spiller
Director, Tecumseh Leadership Center
Camp Tecumseh YMCA Outdoor Center
RR 2, Box 311
Brookston, IN 47923, USA
(317) 564-2898

BLIND GEOMETRY AND TEAMS LACKING DIRECTION

INTRODUCTION

When faced with the challenge of building a group that lacks a structured existence or common sense of purpose, this initiative has been successfully framed to provide an isomorphic experience in the determination of group goals and the consensus process of decision-making. The activity is very effective early in the process of group development to facilitate positive interaction between all group members, while providing the group with a benchmark in balancing group interaction with task completion. With little or no physical contact, this is a non-threatening initiative useful to a variety of groups from ad hoc corporate teams to adolescent peer groups.

GOALS

When presented as described, this initiative provides the group with exposure to the following concepts: (1) establishing effective roles within team parameters, (2) determination of a process to achieve a goal, and (3) consensus value of quality for the team.

SET-UP

The set-up for the activity is similar to the Blind Square initiative. Begin the initiative by explaining that each member of a team carries his/her own notions of group work into the process, as well as a variety of external commitments that affect his/her investment into the group (time, energy, skills, etc.). To represent these "filters," provide each member with a blindfold to be worn during the initiative. Before donning the blindfolds, participants are made aware of their surrounding environmental conditions to ensure safety. After everyone has been blindfolded and they are standing in an amorphous shape (circles provide a frame of reference), circulate among the group with a 50-foot rope, distributing team members randomly along the entire length. The result should be a clump of people, each holding the rope in one hand, with the rope loosely intertwined among the group. The team is now instructed to form a "perfect" square without letting go of the rope or sliding their hands along the rope. Remind the group to exercise caution in stretching the rope to prevent tripping or pulling someone.

SAMPLE PRESENTATION

Have the team gather loosely for the opening instructions. "Each of us builds a lifetime of experiences that help us filter information and form opinions. While this process is quite natural and essential for us, our views are limited only to our exposure. When faced with new or difficult situations, we often filter the facts before us and miss some valuable information. With that in mind, you will all have filters for this activity (pass out blindfolds) to help make the group task more realistic. Before you block out the world of sight, everyone take note of the physical environment around you. Make sure you are aware of all factors which will be useful to you in the safe completion of this activity (point out the major hazards, if any). I will remain in the world of vision to ensure everyone's safety. As you stand where you are, I will place a section of rope in your hand. At no time during the activity should you let go of the rope or slide along the rope. The rope represents the purpose of your team. Who has some idea of what I mean by that statement?" (Typical responses are "because it has no shape" or "because we all have a part in it.") "At this time the task of your team is to create a 'perfect' square with the rope as the perimeter of the shape. The square represents 'direction and focus' for your team, so upon completion of the square, you will have a better idea of how your team copes with the formation of that direction and focus." The team will then begin the process of establishing roles and determining a solution/method to accomplish the task.

LOGISTICS

Blindfolded participants create a manageable but very real safety risk. Pick a large open area with no "surprises" (e.g., stumps, rocks, holes, etc.) and set the tone of the group to ensure that someone doesn't accidentally injure him/herself or someone else. Having an extra staff leader to stand opposite you while the team works the initiative is helpful. Take note of the interaction for valuable discussion material during the debriefing. The group should define their standard of quality by telling you when they feel they have finished.

DEBRIEFING

The absence of sight will propel the participants into the first stage of debriefing as they begin to share what "really" happened. A rotation through each member to state what he/she actually did is a helpful beginning to sort out the confusion and provide a community version of how the activity progressed. Once the facts are agreed upon, the group begins to unravel the meaning of their actions by discussing various leadership styles, roles, and methods of agreement. Gradually participants should be encouraged to reflect upon their individual contributions to the activity and how they relate to the functioning of the team in general. The discussion usually leads to the recognition that each member has a part to play, even if not in the directive leadership of the task. Applying that to normal "working" situations provides an avenue for future development within the team. The creation of strong connections to the clients by using language and structures that are familiar to them makes this activity more effective.

CONTRIBUTOR

John R. Foster, Principal
Education Resource Network
2445 19th, Apt. C
Boulder, CO 80304, USA
(303) 545-9850
(303) 440-7910

MINESHAFT OR THE CORPORATE CLIMB

INTRODUCTION

Since corporate teams can be (on the average) more sedentary and somewhat reluctant (for the most part) to participate in strenuous physical activity, the initiative known as The Wall may seem a bit much for them. This initiative is a reasonable alternative for corporate teams and may also be used as an intermediate lead-in to The Wall for appropriate groups.

GOALS

The goals for this initiative are generally the same as for The Wall in that problem-solving, trust, cooperation, and communication are the principal aspects of teamwork needed to complete this task successfully. As in The Wall, if the group does not anticipate the consequences of their actions, they may be left with one member stranded at the bottom unable to finish the task. Framed in the Corporate Climb isomorph, the point of stepping on one another "to get to the top" enriches the learning.

SET-UP

This initiative is dependent on a specially constructed facility like The Wall. One common way to build the necessary resource is as a platform between two walls. This way one wall acts as a backstop to the other and the platform in between can have a trap door cut in it. (Plans of such an arrangement are available free of charge from this contributor.) The idea behind the initiative is, instead of lifting group members over a 12–14 foot wall, to pass them up through the trap door about 10–12 feet from the ground, like escaping from a small opening in the roof of a mineshaft.

SAMPLE PRESENTATION

The group is gathered inside the structure between the two walls with the roof over their heads. The facilitator begins by discussing a vision that all group members will rise to the top of the corporate climb. Along the way they may step on colleagues to gain higher ground, but will they return to help those that climb behind them? The facilitator continues, explaining that in order to complete this task satisfactorily, the group must end up on top of the structure without going outside of the walls that surround them. (Note: The trap door is hidden and must be discovered!) If desired, the group can be cautioned not to use any props (like nearby ladders or ropes) and can be given a time limit (e.g., pending retirement, if they haven't yet made it to the top). Spotting is necessary as people lift one another up through the opening and participants need to be cautioned not to look upward as they are raised (as heads swing backwards they can bump the edge of the opening as their body is pulled up and through).

LOGISTICS

The lower height (about two feet less than The Wall), coupled with the platform surrounding the opening, permits participants to lie down (thereby protecting lower backs) or squat (using legs instead of the back) and dangle their arms through the opening to lift the last person. The size of the opening can vary according to preference. A one-foot by two-foot opening will accommodate all but the largest individuals. The task is very "do-able" compared with The Wall, as a time limit becomes the pressing concern. Structural constraints (e.g., blindfolds) can be added to increase difficulty. One constraint that has proven especially useful for groups that are dysfunctional around communication is the use of matches as "tickets to speak." Each group member is given one "strike anywhere" match and told that if they have something to say, they must strike the match and may only speak for as long as they can keep the match burning (a few corporations have found this so powerful an experience that the technique has been adopted at certain times in board meetings). The sign of a collaborative team can be when some members begin sharing their matches with others who have something to say but no matches. Quiet members can receive extra matches, while loud ones may not get any.

DEBRIEFING

Debriefing is the same as it might be for The Wall. The almost guaranteed accomplishment of getting everyone on top, once the trap door is found and opened, makes this initiative worthy of providing positive reinforcement to a group who is not doing too well in terms of success. The debrief can also focus on the impact of stepping on others to get to the top and on whether help was given to those who were left behind.

CONTRIBUTOR

Dr. Simon Priest
Director, Corporate Adventure Training Institute
Brock University
St. Catharines, Ontario
Canada L2S 3A1
(905) 688–5550

TEAM TRIANGLE

INTRODUCTION

This initiative is an outgrowth of the Blind Polygon where a blind-folded group must form a particular shape (e.g., a square or triangle) from a continuous piece of rope. It can be used for a wide variety of clientele, but in this example was used as a tool for raising awareness of communication with corporate teams in Australia.

GOAL

The goals for this initiative are: (1) to investigate positive and negative aspects of communication within and among groups, (2) to examine the notion of power and its use in relation to possessing information, and (3) to determine how well group members are empowered to contribute in solving group problems.

SET-UP

If there is a group of about 12 people, break them into three sub-groups (the sub-groups do not need to be the same size, although three people in one sub-group helps if you choose to use the triangle for the team task). The sub-groups are physically separated by designated boundaries that members of each sub-group may not cross. One sub-group is designated as mute, and another sub-group (the one performing the task) is blindfolded. A go-between sub-group is able to fully use all of their faculties. The general idea is that the mute sub-group non-verbally communicates the task to the go-between sub-group, who in turn tell the blind sub-group how to perform the task. Sub-groups may be arranged in a triangle so communication is enhanced by open observation, or structured into a line so that all information must follow a linear pattern through the go-between sub-group.

SAMPLE PRESENTATION

Once the sub-groups are arranged and informed to stay within their boundaries, an introductory statement is made about how groups are typically made up of several sub-groups working on the same project, but speaking different languages (an appropriate isomorph can be framed here, such as data flow from design through engineering to production, or from customer through supervisor to worker). After the whole group is aware that they have been placed into such an arrangement, they are reminded that the mute sub-group must not talk, the go-between sub-group has full use of all faculties, and the blind sub-group must not look. Together, they are to complete a team task. At the start of the initiative, a coiled continuous rope (or another collection of components, depending on the task) is dropped near the blind group and the mute group is provided with written directions. For the triangle team task, these directions can read as follows: "Using all the rope provided, your team must form a perfect equilateral triangle (all three angles = 60 degrees) with all three sides equal in length within a two-inch (5 cm) tolerance. You may untangle the rope, but may not untie any knots which make the rope continuous. Unless there are any questions, you may begin."

LOGISTICS

The task performed with corporate teams is rarely to form a triangle. To increase the isomorphic content of the initiative, corporate teams frequently assemble an object which has relevance to their business. Automotive companies assemble engine or brake components, computer companies assemble hardware components, and service companies build bridges to connect sub-groups.

DEBRIEFING

Process and transfer for this initiative should center on the three original goals (i.e., communication, power, and/or empowerment) and/ or on any issues arising from the observation of the group process. Particular attention may be paid to how sub-groups intra- or inter-communicate, and who in each sub-group assumes pivotal roles as discussion coordinators or "conduits" for the passing of vital data. The usual communication errors (e.g., linking up with names before sending messages to the blindfolded, precision of directions given, everyone speaking at once, lack of paraphrasing to ensure comprehension) are worth debriefing, as there can be feelings of frustration and failure from temporary setbacks. Pre- or post-readings on various communication models may prove useful in relation to this debriefing.

Typically, the initiative has proceeded as follows: The mute sub-group will have little trouble in getting the triangle idea across to the go-between sub-group, but will experience some irritation in explaining the tolerance requirements. Once their message has been successfully passed on, the mute sub-group may begin to divest themselves from the team task ("we've done our bit, we can relax now") or may be ignored by the go-between sub-group ("we've got what we need"). The same shift in power can sometimes be seen when the go-between sub-group has fully explained the task to the blind sub-group. In other cases, a sub-group may wish to retain control over the task by keeping important information to themselves until absolutely necessary to share it. In dysfunctional groups, the blind sub-group members are often treated like "drones" or "pawns" and are only told what to do (i.e., they have very little input to solving any problems which arise along the way). In extreme instances, they are disempowered by being instructed to "shut up and do as you are told." The notion of various types of power and how each can be utilized in a group situation works well as a focus for this debrief.

Regarding problem-solving, one problem that seems to occur time and time again in this initiative is solving the tolerance concern (i.e., how to measure all three sides to equal length within outlined parameters). Blindfolded members will be told to measure the length by a variety of methods (e.g., arm spans, hand widths, shoe lengths) but rarely will they be asked for their ideas. More often than not, the best solution comes from the blind sub-group (closest to the "hands-on" task), who occasionally suggest laying lengths of the rope parallel to see how the sides of the triangle compare. In fact, this is the manner by which the facilitator may check completion of this team task when the group is finished.

CONTRIBUTOR

Dr. Simon Priest
Director, Corporate Adventure Training Institute
Brock University
St. Catharines, Ontario
Canada L2S 3A1
(905) 688–5550

COMPUTER DISINFECTANT

INTRODUCTION

This presentation uses the Nuclear Reactor, or Three Mile Island, activity where an upside down bucket (reactor core) is removed from a designated area (reactor housing) without dropping any radioactive fuel (tennis ball on top of the bucket) by a group of workers (team members) collectively operating a "core removal tool" (bungee cord which can be stretched around the bucket, with a dozen ropes running from the bungee cord to the hands of individual members). Since this type of presentation with corporate teams has little value, several modifications may be made to strengthen its applicability. (Note: To add real consequence to this initiative, it can be conducted around a swimming pool, with appropriate precautions.)

GOAL

This initiative seems to work best at the end of the day, when the team has begun to gel and most major dysfunctions have been identified, reduced, or addressed. The goal is to simulate, as closely as possible, a task that has direct relevance to the group. The observed process is frequently rich in many aspects of teamwork: cooperation, communication, trust, empowerment, risk-taking, support, problem-solving, decision-making, and leadership. In essence, it is a test of how far the group has progressed as a team. In this situation, this activity is prescriptively framed for a computer company.

SET-UP

Place a bucket upside down on a floating platform in the middle of the swimming pool (turn off the filtration system to reduce its movement about and around the pool). Put a cup of granulated chlorine (or other suitable chemical reactant) atop the bucket (which makes for an interesting reaction if spilled). Position at least four hula hoops equidistantly around the edge of the pool. Assume a group of at least 16 members and designate their roles in relation to their actual job responsibilities: The vice-president of Data Management and Computer Systems is in charge of a sub-group of three designers (or more for larger groups) and four directors. Each director is in charge of two (or more) programmers for a total of eight programmers. The programmers are blindfolded and placed as pairs inside a hula hoop at the pool's edge (provide personal flotation devices [PFD's] for any who may be unsure of their swimming ability). The designers are provided with one rubber band (a cross-section of an inner tube large enough to fit around the bucket, but small enough to just barely make it) and four pieces of rope/cord (long enough to stretch across the widest part of the pool). Written directions are provided to the vice-president only (these may or may not be shared with the directors, in keeping with normal company procedures). The vice-president must remain in an office area (within visual and verbal contact of the operation, but unable to physically influence the outcome). Directors may visit the vice-president, and their own pair of programmers, but not those of any other director. Programmers must stay in their hula hoops and no one may enter the swimming pool (except by accident). Designers may go anywhere in the activity area, except the pool.

SAMPLE PRESENTATION

Written directions may read as follows: "You are vice-president in charge of the Data Management and Computer Systems Department for your company. A computer virus (cup) has infected a piece of software (bucket) which is connected (by the floating platform) to many other programs within your company's mainframe computer (swimming pool). In approximately one hour, a time-locked routine will give the virus unimpeded access to all programs within the mainframe. Your team's task is to remove the virus and the infected software (get both cup and bucket out of the pool) without crashing the mainframe (don't spill the contents of the cup), before time runs out. You have at your disposal three designers who have the materials (rubber band and cord) to write a disinfectant utility (create the tool used to remove the bucket and cup). The disinfectant utility is operated from four computer terminals (hula hoops), but the utility requires at least two programmers, working only from their terminals, to run it. Your interface with each pair of programmers is as a director. Since programmers typically have knowledge of what is happening at their terminal only, they are blind to operations at other terminals. No one may enter the computer or touch any part of the infected software or virus until the task is completed. Only designers may touch the raw materials. Once constructed, only blind people may operate the utility. Anyone accidently touching the utility will be blindfolded. You have one hour. Unless there are any questions you can begin now."

LOGISTICS

This is usually a successful challenge for motivated and effective teams. Less capable groups are more likely to experience failure or several setbacks. To reduce the challenge, remove the threat of getting wet by doing the initiative on dry land and permit all personnel free roam around the activity area (except inside the computer). The more cords attached to the rubber band, and/or the more people pulling on them, the easier the task is. To increase the challenge, blindfold the programmers prior to their entering the activity area, so they have little initial comprehension of the task facing their team.

DEBRIEFING

Debriefing ought to focus on issues arising during the initiative. Provided this activity is designed isomorphically to mirror the hierarchy of the group involved, many of the interactions and demonstrated actions will also be realistic representations of actual working behaviors for these people. For example, the stress and pressure created by having to continuously pull hard on the cords while blindfolded leads to certain conflicts among group members. Furthermore, since planning breaks naturally occur in between small successes along the way (such as grabbing the bucket), programmers are sometimes "left holding the bag" as management has yet another meeting to figure out what to do next. The richness of this initiative lends itself to debriefing a broad spectrum of group processes. Most importantly, enjoy!

CONTRIBUTOR

Michael A. Gass, PhD
Department of Kinesiology
New Hampshire Hall
University of New Hampshire
124 Main Street
Durham, NH 03824-3559, USA
(603) 862–2024

Dr. Simon Priest
Director, Corporate Adventure Training Institute
Brock University
St. Catharines, Ontario
Canada L2S 3A1
(905) 688–5550

REFINERY RE-ENGINEERING

INTRODUCTION

Consider the following example from an oil refinery. The company has placed the vast majority of its employees through group initiative programs and has developed teamwork in independent units separated by their different functions. The company is now interested in training members of these units to work cross-functionally with members from other units. In other words, company employees work well within teams, but work poorly among teams. The company's desire for these changes stems from an unusually high spillage of oil within the refinery.

As crude oil undergoes the refining process, it is passed from unit to unit. Spills along the way are blamed on others, since units can shirk the responsibility to other units or to other shifts. To make matters worse, the company pays higher wages (overtime) to clean up the spills than it does to refine the oil. The obvious Total Quality Management issue here is the personal financial incentive to spill oil versus the loss of revenues from lowered output (not to mention the ecological concern). The solution might seem quite simple, but the presence of a strong union and stubborn management make resolution tough. Here are seven steps to creating the isomorphic frame.

1. From several thorough diagnostic interviews, the following needs were stated and ranked in the following order:

   a. Resolution of the oil spill situation.
   b. Improved cooperation between union and management.
   c. Development of cross-functional team work.
   d. Better communication between shifts.
   e. Enhanced trust among members of different units.
   f. Increased risk-taking for employees (by speaking out and sharing ideas).

2. Selection of a metaphoric adventure experience was difficult for facilitators due to the following reasons: Since group initiatives had served the company well, they wanted further teamwork activities; however, since the novelty of these activities had already been fully exhausted, the company wanted something more extensive and exciting. The high ropes course was chosen as the vehicle for achieving teamwork, although it is not normally team-oriented. In fact, unless a high-performing team has been created prior to its use, the ropes course can have devastating impacts on teamwork. Without the supportive atmosphere that typically accompanies an effective functional team, the ropes course can turn into a destructive macho competition.

On the positive side, the high ropes course experience can be modified to be more team-oriented by having clients belay each other (rather than placing that responsibility on facilitators or technicians) and by devising extra tasks within the activity that have a group problem-solving requirement. In this particular case, the high ropes course provided opportunities to work on risk-taking and trust. With teamwork modifications, it would add communication and cooperation to the list. However, the needs of cross-function and oil spillage demanded some isomorphic modification.

3. Successful resolution of the training and development issue was identified as getting management and union to cooperate toward fixing the high incidence of oil spills. The isomorphic frame would have to duplicate this situation with an opportunity for positive outcome. If this did indeed happen during the activity, then the results would have to reflect and reward this. On the other hand, if the outcomes were negative setbacks (arising from the ineffectiveness of the group or their inability to put differences aside and work together), then the results would have to hold consequences similar to those faced in the future of the workplace (e.g., layoffs, pay cuts).

4. The isomorphic framework was strengthened by transforming the high ropes course into a mirror image of the refinery. Each element of the ropes course became a refining function in the process (e.g., cracking, distillation) and the activity was renamed Refinery Re-engineering.

The pilot program for this company was conducted with the unit supervisors from each shift. Ten of these employees were salaried engineers, while 10 others were hourly technicians. Two representatives from the union and two from upper management were also present. Supervisors were assigned to an element of the ropes course which best represented the function of the unit that they supervised at work. For each element or function, the first supervisor was placed on the high ropes course (on shift) while the second was on the ground (off shift) supporting the first with a belay. A large supply of tennis balls represented crude oil and was to be placed into buckets (10 per barrel of oil). The task given this group was to transport the buckets of balls (barrels of crude oil) through each element of the ropes course (refining function) in order. The group was given $100 and told that real money would be used to buy lunch at noon. The isomorphic frame continued:

Crude oil costs $10 per barrel ($1/ball), while refined oil brings in $50 per barrel ($5/ball) after being passed through the complete 10-step refinery process. Each step of the refinery process costs $1 per barrel (10 cents/ball). So in summary, one barrel of crude oil will cost $10 to buy and $10 to refine, but will bring a $30 profit. In addition, spilled oil will cost $20 per barrel ($2/ball) to clean up. Furthermore, if oil is spilled at the start, no processing costs will be lost. However, if oil is spilled near the end, then the total processing costs for each stop to the point of spillage will be wasted (seven steps = $7). In either case, the cost of the crude oil will also be forfeited.

The 20 supervisors were responsible for passing balls through the ropes course, with each person repeating their element several times with many buckets of balls. The management and union representatives were responsible for cleaning up dropped balls, buying crude oil, and selling refined oil. After one hour, the shifts changed and supervisory roles were exchanged, with union and management representatives continuing in their combined roles. After a second hour, the books were balanced, and the funds left were used to purchase lunch.

After lunch, time was devoted to re-engineering the process. Certain variables were fixed. They included market prices, number of steps in the refinery process, and types of functions in each step. However, the manner in which oil was handled and who performed each function was open to negotiation within the group. Once again, the group was given $100 and told that real money would be used to buy dinner that night. During the late afternoon, the re-engineered process was put into action with a pair of one-hour shifts. At the end of the two hours, the books were again balanced and leftover funds were used to purchase dinner. An evening debrief was conducted.

5. In reviewing client motivation, the frame sounded a bit weak, so facilitators added some imagery in the form of titles. Each element of the ropes course and the equipment used to belay were labeled with the names of actual facilities and tools back at the real refinery. At no time was the need to work together explicitly stated as the reason for being

there. However, teamwork was an obvious and implicit component of the activity. A double check of appropriate content and relationships with the company trainers gave the impression the frame was suitable.

6. As the experience was conducted, several minor revisions were necessary. Facilitators had to change a few labels as their interpretations of functions were slightly off. One advantage to this revision was that clients were more closely connected to the frame, since they were able to tailor it to fit their comprehension of reality. As the frame was explained, many group members were quick to pick up on transfer points between functions where potential for spillage was high. Some were even able to equate this to their new roles as risk analyzers under a total quality approach. A few noted that key problem points were equivalent and similar to those in their real refinery. Later in the re-engineering portion, they undertook the responsibility of fixing those same problems. Overall, the morning project showed a loss of over half the original starting funds. This amounted to about $2 per person remaining for food. Needless to say, the meal was sparse at best. On the other hand, the afternoon project brought a healthy profit of almost $25 per person. Dinner was a banquet with free-flowing drinks. Apparently, the client's re-engineering worked for the better. In fact, it worked so well in this case that facilitators ran out of money to buy refined oil.

7. In the debrief, clients had found the metaphor to be obvious and powerful. Management and union had worked hand in hand to address the oil spillage. Since the activity was almost identical to work, these representatives returned to the refinery confident that they could work together to do so again. Lastly, the objectives of cooperation, communication, trust, and risk-taking were met.

CONTRIBUTOR

Dr. Simon Priest, Director
Corporate Adventure Training Institute
Brock University
St. Catharines, Ontario
Canada L2S 3A1
(905) 688–5550

CHINA SYNDROME

INTRODUCTION

Objective: To have a team of people control a "nuclear meltdown" at a power plant by placing a container of control material into the reactor shaft.

Area: An opaque barrier is erected six feet high by 20 feet wide. Four feet from the center of the barrier on one side, a 2x2 square (or similar sized circle) is placed on the ground. This is the back side of the activity, the reactor shaft. All further activity takes place on the front side.

An area is marked off with rope or other border material on the front side, beginning with a straight line parallel to the barrier, four feet away from it. The line extends 10 feet along the center of the barrier. Two side lines are then extended back at right angles away from the barrier for at least 20 feet. All participants must stay within this area during the activity.

Props: The group is given three 8-foot 4x4's, one 12-foot 4x4, six to eight short pieces of rope for lashing, one 35-foot piece of rope, a cinder block, and a #10 can full of water (control material).

SET-UP

The group is ushered into the activity area (loading dock) and told the following situation: "A meltdown has occurred in the reactor. A hasty work area and barrier have been erected to attempt to contain it. Only one expert on meltdowns is available within hours of the power plant and has been flown in to assist" (this person is designated by the facilitator and steps aside for the time being). The group is instructed to discuss the situation among themselves until the expert arrives.

The facilitator takes the "expert" aside and explains the details of the situation. "The group must, within the given time limit, get the control material over the barrier and into the reactor shaft designated by a 2'x2' square on the ground without spilling a drop, as the amount is precisely calculated. The material must be placed securely within the square without spilling and stand upright without support. If it spills or misses the area, the group must try again until successful. They are able to use to use only the resources described above and must remain on the loading dock at all times. No one may step or reach beyond the line drawn four feet from the barrier wall. This is the 'safe' zone for operating."

The facilitator then asks if the expert has any questions. No one may ask the facilitator for clarification during the problem. They must address the expert.

SOLUTION

The group uses the resources to create a structure that can transport the material into the shaft without anyone reaching or stepping outside the boundaries.

APPLICABILITY

This is a challenging initiative that requires planning, problem-solving, and cooperation. One of its strengths is the number of people who must be involved in different but supportive tasks at any one time. It works well with organizations that have cross-functional roles that support one common product or service. It addresses the issues of alternate leadership and support roles as task groups come together to solve the problem.

CONTRIBUTOR

Rob Rubendall
Elderhostel, Inc.
75 Federal Street
Boston, MA 02110, USA
(617) 426-7788

USING "TARGET SPECIFICATIONS" FOR BUSINESS POPULATIONS

INTRODUCTION

The following initiative was specifically created as a metaphor for the difficulty in achieving a specification target, such as the number of correct invoices processed per week, a dimensional specification (e.g., 31.05 +/– 0.4 mm), the number of completed orders per month, etc. This activity works well for cross-functional organizations, engineering teams, or other groups comprised of members with different talents or skills. An example of a cross-functional organization (in this case, a medical team) would consist of doctors, surgeons, charge nurses, administrators, housekeepers, and staff members, compared to a non-cross-functional team consisting of a single entity, such as all B-shift ICU nurses.

GOALS

This initiative emphasizes the following: (1) the need for cooperation and communication between team members, especially in situations where one team member may be disadvantaged due to location, technical abilities, familarity with a process or piece of equipment, etc.; and (2) the need for flexibility and perseverance when specifications change.

SET-UP

A single blindfolded player (the "supplier") stands in the center of a 20–30-foot diameter circle. The remaining team members (ideally 4–8 people) each grasp "the target," a hula-hoop or soft rope loop about three feet in diameter. The supplier is given a series of items to throw towards the target. Typical items include beachballs, tennis balls, racket balls, water balloons, red playground balls, frisbees, kooshballs, paper airplanes, nerf footballs, flexible cloth frisbees, foam sections, paper plates, and (the author's favorite) a rubber chicken. The target team can move and attempts to position themselves so that the thrown object passes through the center of the target. Verbal communication is allowed (and encouraged) between the team and the supplier, even before the activity begins.

SAMPLE PRESENTATION

"Your engineering group has recently been assigned the task of designing a high-technology device (such as a disk drive) with tight specification tolerances on several critical components. In order to meet the challenging specifications of this product, you must form a project team and closely interface with your supplier. Communication is largely verbal (analogous to using the phone as the primary communication tool) except for several prototypes which the supplier will be sending."

(After several items have been thrown, offer the team a smaller target and report to them that research has indicated that a tighter specification tolerance is required on the remaining equipment to be shipped from the supplier. It is probable that additional communication and cooperation will be necessary to complete this design task.)

VARIATIONS

Thrown Objects—Always use soft items that will not cause injury if they happen to contact a team member rather than the target. Additional items include: party balloons, inflated beach toys, air-filled garbage bags or baggies, weather balloons, knotted cloth rags, socks, or gloves and pillows.

The Rubber Chicken—For this object, the team can only provide information on their location to the supplier by "clucking" or making other chicken sounds. This may be analogous to translating technical information in a foreign language.

Environment—Try playing in a pool at various water depths. The team will have to react quicker and work hard to overcome the resistance of the water.

Blindfolds—Try blindfolding the target team and using a sighted supplier. This approach quickly shifts the responsibility for a successful catch from several players (the team) to a single individual (the supplier). This is analogous to a baseball pitcher trying to hit the bat with his pitch. Notice how easy it is to blame a single player (scapegoat) in this situation. This is a good debriefing subject.

You can also try adding a blindfolded team member with each thrown object and notice how increasingly difficult it is to react. Also notice how dependent the team becomes on the remaining sighted players.

Target Size—Use a smaller hula hoop or rope circle to increase the difficulty of this initiative.

DEBRIEFING

The main debriefing issues here are the method of communication between the team and the supplier (one player vs. the entire team), the alterations made for various objects (e.g., weight of the object, avoidance of the water balloon, wind effects), and the effect of changing the specification target size. Additional discussion is appropriate for each of the variations presented above.

CONTRIBUTOR

Jim Cain
Teamplay
456 Dewey Street
Churchville, NY 14428,USA
(716) 293-3771

2B OR KNOT 2B

INTRODUCTION

Although some adventure initiatives require physical attributes such as strength, balance, flexibility, or mobility, here is an activity that requires no physical exertion and yet successfully helps group members understand their own problem-solving and decision-making skills. The ropes used in this activity can be thought of as metaphors for difficult tasks, computer networks, the information superhighway, the members of a group or team, or even the individual tasks of a much larger project.

GOALS

This initiative emphasizes: (1) the process involved in making a group decision, (2) individual problem-solving techniques, and (3) the importance of listening to each team member and coming to a team consensus.

SET-UP

This activity uses of six rope segments, each 10 feet long. Use a variety of rope colors, thicknesses, or textures to add visual variety to the puzzle. Take a single piece of rope and tie the two ends together to form a loop. Do the same with four more of the rope segments to form a total of five separate loops. Now take the remaining rope and pass it through the other loops so that this final rope will join the others together. Finally, tie the two ends of this last rope together. Now place the completed rope tangle on the ground or a table so that all team members can easily see it. Interweave the rope segments so that it is difficult to see which rope is holding the others together.

SAMPLE PRESENTATION

"A very serious economic problem has surfaced that is greatly affecting the economy of a small country. Your team has been chosen to investigate this problem. You should be aware that the problem appears to be composed of several factors, one of which is by far the most important. Your team's task is to investigate this problem and make a group decision about which portion is the most important (i.e., which rope holds all the others together)."

LOGISTICS

Team members are not allowed to touch the ropes during their decision-making process. The object here is to determine which rope holds all the others together. Encourage everyone to decide for themselves which rope is holding the others together, or alternatively, which ropes are not holding the others together (process of elimination). Work towards group consensus.

VARIATIONS

Rope—Colorful ropes of various sizes and textures are easy to distinguish. This activity can be made more difficult by using several ropes of the same color, or ultimately difficult by using all ropes of the same color. Even the most colorful ropes, however, will be difficult to distinguish with limited lighting (just another way of showing how an easy task can be made even more challenging without the proper tools). Ten feet is about the right length for 1/2-inch-diameter rope. You can use less for twine and small rope. You can also use more than six segments (four is fairly easy; eight is difficult).

Knots—Using a variety of knots to join the ropes together can be helpful in teaching basic rope work to the group. You can also use chain links, metal rings, or splice work to join the rope ends.

Orientation—This activity can be used on the ground or on a table. It can even be hung on a wall for large groups to view. The important point is to tangle the ropes together so that it is no longer obvious which rope is holding the others together.

Decision-Making—Try taking votes on which rope is most likely to be holding the others together; then have team members work to convince the others why their choice is correct.

DEBRIEFING

Debriefing issues include the evaluation of the problem-solving techniques used by each team member, the methods used to reach group consensus, the process of elimination, and the relationship of the ropes to the metaphor selected.

CONTRIBUTOR

Jim Cain
Teamplay
468 Salmon Creek Road
Brockport, NY 14420-9761, USA
(716) 637-0328

CORPORATE LADDER

INTRODUCTION

This initiative can be used with corporate teams or other work groups. Its purpose is to explore communication styles, layers of management, and relationships. It addresses current paradigms or creates new ways of achieving success (i.e., reorganization, delegation of power, trusting the system). This initiative also simulates the pressure caused by competition either within or outside the organization. It is best used with groups that have: (1) contracted to work on systemic communication problems, (2) working knowledge of a high element, and (3) members who feel comfortable being blindfolded.

SET-UP

This initiative uses the rope ladder and a dynamic belay. This should be set up ahead of time according to your course specifications. Harnesses need to be available for the climber and belayer.

This initiative is set up for a two-person dynamic belay and/or a five-person belay team (i.e., a primary and secondary belay, an anchor for each belayer, and a rope handler). This can be adjusted according to the belay techniques used on your course. A facilitator can be in one of the belay positions, depending on the expertise of the group.

Set-up also includes teaching belaying if this has not been done before. Due to the complexity of the communication process of this initiative, it is suggested not to use this as the first high initiative.

GOALS

1. For the group of participants to explore their role in achieving success, as well as establishing what success is for them.
2. Explore stereotypical communication styles within organizations, as well as any new patterns that aid in the "success/failure" of the group.
3. Explore issues regarding competition and how that may help or hinder the group.

SAMPLE PRESENTATION

"In this day of job uncertainty, corporate shuffling, quality improvement, inverted triangles, self-directed teams, and flat-lined management, there are many changes occurring in the workplace. Despite this precarious atmosphere, or because of it, there are still those you willing to climb the corporate ladder. Today, one or more of you will be given the opportunity to climb this ladder. At this time, I need the group to choose someone who is willing to take this challenge." (Hopefully the group will choose someone at this point.)

"As those of you who are in a corporate culture know, sometimes climbing the ladder is difficult and we are not always able to foresee what is in store for us. So, at this time, I will need for our climber to put on this bandanna. There are several other jobs to be filled. I will read the job and the group can decide who they believe best fits each position:

CEO: 'Primary belay.' All are silent while you speak. You are ultimately responsible for the climb and descent of your employee.

BOARD OF DIRECTORS: 'Secondary belay.' Support the CEO and be there if the CEO gives up or is distracted (a facilitator may need to play one of these two positions depending on how your facility utilizes the belay techniques).

PRESIDENT: Anchors the CEO.

VICE PRESIDENT: Anchors the Board of Directors.

EXECUTIVE SECRETARY: Rope handler. In charge of preventing any entanglements of the Executive Team.

DIRECTOR: Gives the manager directions on how they believe climber could best accomplish the 'Corporate Ladder.'

MANAGER: Gives directions to climber after listening to Director.

COMPETITOR: You are jealous of your co-worker's accomplishments. You do not want him/her to succeed. Use statements like 'You'll never make it.' (Facilitator: If the group is responsible enough, this person can be creative with their jeers. Use your own judgment. Falls caused by a competitor are realistic and can be processed positively. Also, this role can be set up as a real life competitor for this work group (i.e., Hospital A versus Hospital B, or it can be set up positively as 'Who of you is competitive and enjoys challenging others?').

ENCOURAGER: You cheer and give encouragement but do not give directions.

SUPPORT STAFF: Spot and hold the ladder if the climber asks for that type of support." (Use anyone who is left. If there are not enough people left to spot, you will need to get the director, manager, and encourager to help with this task.)

DEBRIEFING

The following topics may arise:

1. Communication: Everyone speaking at once and not listening to the CEO; others giving directions; the competitor being louder than others (especially louder than the encourager).
2. Success: Find out what it means for the group to "make it to the top." Is there any reward up there? How does it feel to come down? (Facilitator can set it up so that climber is sighted on the way down or rappels from the initiative.)
3. Competition: How is negative feedback or reinforcement used with this group? Is negative feedback "louder" than positive? How did individual climbers deal with competition?
4. Creative Problem-Solving: Did the group deviate from the perceived rules? Was there any committee meeting or planning meetings to aid or hinder the group? Who called the meetings? Did anyone give up power for the betterment of the task or safety of the climber? Was there reorganization?
5. Trusting the System: Did the group follow the rules to the letter and was there trust in the system? Is this how this group normally functions?
6. Vision: Did the group have the same vision? Was this communicated to the blind climber and vice-versa?
7. Checking In with Each Participant: It is valuable information for the group to hear how each job has different demands and how those relate to that individual.

CONTRIBUTOR

Bobbie Williams
Community Hospital North
7150 Clearvista Drive
Indianapolis, IN 46256, USA
(317) 841-5197

THE BRIDGE

INTRODUCTION

This initiative is designed for business groups, but is probably appropriate for all groups. Very often a business group will take on additional work even though they are currently overloaded. In doing so, they often spread themselves so thin that they are unable to accomplish anything very successfully. Very often a team will make no attempt to prioritize their current work or eliminate current projects when they take on new ones.

GOAL

The goal of this initiative is to get work groups to prioritize their work and eliminate tasks or projects that are preventing them from performing the work that is most critical to their success.

SET-UP

The set-up is to have the entire group identify all the projects or tasks on which they are currently working. They are then asked to reach consensus on the actual percentage they could successfully accomplish. This "percentage of the whole" becomes the critical number. Their goal will be to eliminate the less critical or unnecessary tasks. Each project or task is written on an index card, one project to a card. Each card is taped to a carpet square after any duplicates are eliminated. The team is lined up behind a line drawn on the floor or ground. The team is given the carpet squares with projects or index cards attached to them. They are told they are on a ledge that is slowly breaking away from the mountain and will completely crumble in five minutes. (The time is variable but should not be too long so that the group has to make some quick decisions.) They must move to safety. Safety is a new ledge drawn on the ground some distance from the ledge on which the team is standing. The new ledge can only withstand the weight of all the team members and the number of projects of squares that the team determined earlier. The team can use the carpet squares as a bridge but they can only be laid end to end in a straight line. They can not be overlapping. As the team walks to safety, the last person in line picks up the tiles and carries them to or hands them to the other team members on the ledge. The remaining tiles are left behind on the crumbling ledge.

CONTRIBUTOR

Howard Rosenberg
Director, Organization Development
Providian Corporation
680 4th Avenue
Louisville, KY 40232, USA

SCHOOL POPULATIONS

TEAM SKI

INTRODUCTION

This adapted Trolley/Team Ski initiative was used in a summer camp setting of 33 participants ages 18–23. The framework of the activity was structured to parallel their workplace situation. Communication and cooperation between administration and counselors were poor. A pre-program survey identified the group's major difficulties as: (1) a lack of respect for the chain of command, and (2) the prevalent attitude that "everyone else's job is easier than mine." These characteristics are not uncommon in many work environments.

OBJECTIVES

This initiative was structured to emphasize:
1. Open communication between administration and counselors.
2. Recognizing that each role has its own set of difficulties and challenges (no job is "a piece of cake").
3. Identifying that a group is in control of the decision to work together or not work together.
4. Realizing the natural consequences of the decision to either work together or not work together.

SETTING THE STAGE

To better meet the objectives and sustain the metaphor, the administrators are asked to participate as team members. The facilitators randomly choose two individuals from each team to be the coaches of that team. Facilitators then announce they will only answer questions from the coaches and the facilitator's decisions are policy. Because of the large size of some groups, not all comments and activities can be seen and remembered for processing. Therefore, we suggest videotaping the initiative and reviewing the tape with the group during processing.

SET-UP

A detailed construction of a Team Ski or Trolley can be found in the Project Adventure publication, *Silver Bullets* (Rohnke, 1984, p. 118). This adaptation consists of sinking an eye bolt in the ends of each ski and using small industrial carabineers to connect the skis together. Instead of drilling holes and attaching permanent rope handles, we use heavy-duty staples on the skis so we can vary the presentation strength, number, and length of handles used.

- Divide participants into equal teams. In a large, open area facilitators establish a starting point, mid-point, and finish line. Each team is given a set of Team Skis along with a bag of cut string and dowels.
- Two individuals from each team are chosen as coaches and receive instructions from the facilitators. Coaches are directed to answer the teams' questions as best they can. If coaches are stumped, they can ask the facilitators for clarification and relay this information back to their team.
- The coaches from each team receive a written copy of the following information:

OBJECTIVE: GET YOUR TEAM TO THE FINISH LINE

Rules: Half of your team will start at the first line. They must stand on the Team Ski without any body parts touching the ground. The group starting at line one will travel as a team to the second line and pick up the other half of their team. As an entire team, all standing on the Team Ski, they will travel to the finish line. Once the entire ski has come across the finish line, the team will receive information for Phase II of this race.

STRINGS AND DOWELS

1. The dowels must be held in the hands (one dowel per hand).
2. The string end not connected to the dowels must be tied to a staple on each Team Ski.

TOUCHES

1. FOR THE COACHES: Any time a foot or body part touches the ground and the group doesn't call the touch on themselves,

the COACH MUST CALL THE TOUCH. The group then must go back to the starting line and start over again. If this occurs after the start from line two, the team goes back to line two to start over.

2. If the team calls the touch on themselves, they must go back three paces. The coach will count the three paces back.

As each team crosses the finish line, their coaches will receive the Phase II written instructions. Coaches of Team A receive only the Team A instructions, etc.

TEAM SKI PHASE II

Team A: Following the same rules, you should connect your skis to Team B.

Team B: Following the same rules, you should connect your skis to Team C.

Team C: Following the same rules, you should connect your skis to Team B.

METAPHOR CONNECTIONS

Initiative	Summer Camp Situation
Coaches	Administrators
Facilitators—set parameters of initiative, give instructions and choose coaches.	Board of Directors—sets goals and hires administration.
Coaches are responsible for directing team skiers and communicating policy as facilitators.	Administration is responsible for directing counselors and upholding policy as by set by the board.
If a coach has to call a touch, it is penalized more severely than if skiers call their own touch.	When counselors keep themselves to standards and rule, there is less intervention by administration.
Communication and coordination in attaining goals become more difficult as the number of skiers increases.	Communication and cordination in attaining goals become more difficult due to the large number of camp staff.

Demands on the coaches by the team skiers are illustrated (asking for guidance, suggesting various courses of action, etc.) all at the same time.	Demands on the administration by the camp staff are great (30 + people asking for guidance, suggesting various courses of action, requesting time off) all at the same time.

PROCESSING ISSUES

This initiative is structured to emphasize that communication is affected by group size. Processing can include comparing communication effectiveness in Phase I with that in Phase II. Exploring the similarities and differences between each phase will focus the group on issues pertinent to the objectives.

These issues include: (1) the ability to empathize with people in different roles, and (2) the acknowledgement that, individually, members do have a choice of how a team works together.

Group involvement can be fostered by asking some open-ended questions. Examples include:

1. As you started the first part of the race, coaches, what were you thinking? Team, what were you thinking?
2. Of the two phases, in which was it easiest to experience success? How so?
3. Did it take a conscious effort to work together?

The wide array of comments made by participants during this initiative can provide an abundant source of processing information. Keep your ears open and go with the flow. Comments like these may lead you in the right direction:

> Coaches: "I'd rather be on skis."
> "Hey! Who's giving the orders here?"
>
> Skiers: "Everybody shut up and listen to the coaches!"
> "We can't hear back here. Let us know what's going on."

CONTRIBUTORS

Brian Welsh
Program Director
9310 West R. Avenue
Kalamazoo, MI 49009, USA

Michele A. Santucci
Graduate Intern
9310 West R. Avenue
Kalamazoo, MI 49009, USA

GOALS, BARRIERS, AND RESOURCES

INTRODUCTION

This initiative can be used with a wide variety of metaphors. It is well suited for addressing the issues of reaching for a goal, stumbling and/ or building the blocks to that goal, and the resources available to reach that goal. I used it successfully with a community group who had the goal of trying to set up an initiatives/ropes course-based program.

LOGISTICS

This activity is commonly referred to as Here to There and requires disks about one foot in diameter. Cardboard is okay, but plywood is more permanent. The number of disks should be half the number of participants plus one. For example, if there are 10 participants, there should be 6 disks (10/2 = 5, plus 1 = 6). Participants start behind one line, and, using only the disks, they must get everyone and the disks across a second line without touching the ground. The distance between the lines generally depends on the functioning level of the group. It should be far enough that the disks, acting as stepping stones, do not reach the whole distance (i.e., disks have to be passed forward). Other rules include: (1) The disks and people can only move forwards, not backwards, (2) before the first person crosses the far line, the last person has to have left the starting line, and (3) if anyone touches the ground there are consequences. These consequences depend on the group. They may include: (1) The group starts over, (2) the person who touched the ground is blindfolded or loses the use of a hand, or (3) certain people or the whole group become mute. Use your intuition and imagination!

There are no serious safety concerns with most populations. However, for some incest survivors, prolonged close contact may be difficult or inhibiting.

SAMPLE PRESENTATION

"Let's have everyone stand over here (behind the first line). You all have the goal of setting up an initiative-based program in the community. The second line represents that program (show them the second line). You as a group need to get from here to there. Your resources are these disks and the group. In between the lines are the pitfalls and obstacles that will make it challenging to reach the goal of developing your initiative-based program (at this point have the group identify some of these obstacles). If anyone touches the ground there will be consequences. (That allows for creative responses to the group process.) You can pass the disks forward but *not backwards* and the first person cannot cross the line over there until the first person has left the starting area."

DEBRIEFING

I begin the debrief by asking the participants what worked well in the process and how they would do it differently next time. It may be necessary to keep the focus on the process and away from the physical solutions. Quite often someone will want to know whether other groups do it the same way or how they did compared with other groups (ease, speed, etc.). It is useful to bring the focus back to the group and away from comparisons. Humor works well (e.g., "most groups do it in a tenth of the time you did it, with both hands tied behind their backs," etc. until they see the absurdity of the answer). Help the group see what parallels there are between the activity and their community/group situation or their personal lives. "What was the activity like for individuals? Did anyone get frustrated? At what point? What did you do about it? Is that a familiar feeling/situation for you?" Help the group examine parallels between consequences in the activity and real-life situations. For example, if someone is blindfolded, it may be similar to someone not having access to all the information in a community project. How is that dealt with currently in the community? What could or should be done differently? It is useful to end with concrete ideas for improving the group's and individuals' strategies in the real-life situation or in future initiatives.

CONTRIBUTOR

Deb Piranian
Health and Education Services
Colorado Outward Bound School
945 Pennsylvania
Denver, CO 80203, USA
(303) 873-0880

THE SPIDER'S WEB
AS A METAPHOR FOR RULES
AND CONFRONTING BROKEN RULES

INTRODUCTION

This initiative is part of a one-day ropes course experience used in two separate one-week programs for training college students who are Safety and Security Officers and Resident Assistants. This activity is an experiential component used near the end of their week to address the difficulty in confronting peers when they see rules being broken. Both groups have said this is the most difficult part of their positions.

GOALS

This initiative provides opportunities for five things to happen: (1) to put the rule enforcers in a situation where they may not like or agree with the rules, (2) to test their reactions to those rules, (3) to discuss their feelings about confronting peers, (4) to experience effective (and maybe ineffective) ways to approach a peer who is caught breaking the rules, and (5) to relate how the relationship of the team members makes the job easier or harder.

SET-UP

The Spider's Web rope is tied and crisscrossed between two fixed poles (trees) allowing enough usable space for each participant to make it through one of the openings created by the crossed ropes. The discussion of the web and its meaning takes place before the students begin the initiatative.

SAMPLE PRESENTATION

Participants are asked to gather on one side of the web. "This web represents some of the challenges you will face on the job this school year. What are some difficulties you anticipate facing?" (Typical responses include: "long hours," "discipline, especially if it's your friend," "getting people interested in your programs," etc.) "This side of the web is the beginning of the school year. All of you standing safely on the other side is the end of the school year. What things can the people in this group do for you that will help you be successful in your job?" (Answers might be: "listen and give advice," "talk directly to me if there is a problem," "help me out if I ask," etc.) "Because each of you is unique, with your own personal strengths and challenges, each hole is available to only one of you to pass through. There is one rule in this initiative that will represent the rules you must follow and enforce during the school year: No touching of any of the ropes or poles (trees) by any member of the group is allowed at any time. Consequences for breaking this rule are that everyone must begin again. Just as there is no one to tell you what to do when you're on the job, I will not interfere in any way unless I see something unsafe happening. Any questions?" The group then proceeds to solve the Spider's Web.

DEBRIEFING

Questions I might ask include: "On a scale from 1–10 how successful were you? What accounts for the different (or similar) opinions on your success? Were they using different criteria? What was the most difficult part of this activity? What was helpful when you got to that point? What was not helpful? How is this similar to your job? What strengths did you notice in your teammates? How will those strengths be helpful in your job? Why did I say the passing through the web is most similar to the passing through the school year, not just one day on the job?" (As leaders they are always role models, not just on the job). Somewhere along this line of discussion the topic of sticking to the original rules comes up. If the group was briefed well, had some trust-building, team-building lead-up activities, and wanted to be successful at this initiative, they will find some answers and support to the challenges they will face on their jobs.

CONTRIBUTOR

Nancy B. Mathias, Associate Director
Center for Leadership Development
St. Norbert College
De Pere, WI 54115, USA
(414) 337–4040

TOXIC WASTE DISPOSAL: ACTIVE LISTENING SKILLS; COOPERATIVE GROUP EFFORT

INTRODUCTION

The objective for the group is to place three toxic waste "canisters" in the "disposal silo." By manipulating the jaws of the "canister disposal crane," each canister can be picked up, moved to the disposal silo, and placed inside the silo. If a canister is knocked over, the group must put on protective suits and headgear; verbal communication is not possible with the protective headgear in place. This initiative addresses positive listening skills, poor listening behaviors, and coordinating group effort to accomplish a common goal.

GOALS

The emphasis of this activity is two-fold: (1) to increase participant awareness of active listening skills, and (2) to practice these skills. Some of these skills can include:

1. Maintaining eye contact between the speaker and listener.
2. Allowing the speaker to talk without interruptions.
3. Extending non-verbal listening skills.
4. Staying focused on the speaker.
5. Asking questions related to the present conversation.
6. Paraphrasing the speaker's thoughts.
7. Not prejudging or disqualifying the speaker's thoughts.

It is also important to create an atmosphere for open exchange and consideration of individual ideas culminating in an agreed-upon group plan of action.

SET-UP

An automobile inner tube is suspended by ropes from 4 to 6 trees or posts; another set of ropes is tied to the inner tube and laid out on the ground. Three fireplace-sized logs are stood upright and placed approximately two feet apart. A large trash container or a 55-gallon drum serves as the disposal silo.

Before presenting this activity, have the participants list indicators that show someone is actively listening to them when they speak. Ask the group to present behaviors that indicate that they are not being listened to while talking. Have the group also consider the linkage between active listening and coordinated group action.

SAMPLE PRESENTATION

"Hearing, listening, communicating, and agreeing are important parts of group activity. In this challenge, each one of those skills is tested.

You are toxic waste disposal experts. Your job is to place each toxic waste canister in the disposal silo. You cannot touch the canisters; instead you must use the disposal crane. The crane can only be operated by manipulating the free ends of the ropes. Toxic fumes are held in the canisters, but they will escape if a canister is tipped over. If a canister tips over, you must each put on your contamination suits and headgear. Because of the nature of the headgear, it is impossible to communicate verbally with the contamination suits on. The protective suits are only effective for five minutes."

DEBRIEFING

Reconsider the indicators the group identified that show someone is listening and the behaviors that indicate that words are not being heard. Participants can discuss the indicators they observed during the activity. Reflect upon the process of group decision-making. Some leading questions that can be asked include:

1. Do people shut off lines of communication unknowingly?
2. How do you let people know your concern over not being heard?
3. Is it hard or easy to repair a broken line of communication?
4. Are you willing to communicate everything to everyone?
5. Do you refuse to communicate some things to anyone?
6. What role does fear play in communication of your feelings, thoughts, and ideas?
7. What processes did the group employ in reaching its plan of action?

8. What role did individual behaviors play in the way the plan of action was implemented?
9. How was the plan of action affected by the absence of verbal communication?

CONTRIBUTOR

Richard B. Chernov, Director
Camp Birch Trail for Girls, Inc.
6570 Regal Manor Drive
Tucson, AZ 85715, USA
(602) 529-9358

THE WEB OF ACADEMIA

INTRODUCTION

The following is an example of an initiative intended to focus the attention of the group on problems they experience daily at work. The members of the group were all employees in a university's office of external relations. This staff contained a very diverse pool of career interests and abilities based on the very nature of their office's complex role within the university. The low ropes course element utilized in this example is commonly referred to as the Spider's Web.

GOALS

The educational objectives of this activity are: (1) to draw attention to the possibility that, within their office, particular individuals may be better suited for specific projects that are initiated by another staff member, and (2) both technical and emotional support are very important in assisting colleagues as they venture into unexplored avenues in their work.

SAMPLE PRESENTATION

"You have all heard that this relatively young university, growing by leaps and bounds, has just announced the opening of two positions in each department. The entire university, as represented by this Web of Academia is comprised of many departments, symbolized by the openings in the web. It may be much more difficult to secure a stable position in some departments than in others.

Once two people have passed through the same opening, that department is filled and the rest of the group must find where their talents can be utilized in other departments. For those in departments, there is a restriction that they only support their comrades still in the job market by assisting from within the confines of the university. In other words, if you get into a department, you must stay on that side of the web.

I shall act as personnel to ensure that the person trying to get into each department is right for the position. Hence, if I should notice people brushing against the departmental borders of the web, I will suggest that they seek another position and declare the opening for any other interested candidates.

Because you all want the university to be successful, you recognize the need to get every one of these talented people into a department somewhere within the Web of Academia. Feel free to put a plan together, and if there are no questions on your challenge, you may begin now."

DEBRIEFING

Although the group had to deal with several occasions in which an individual touched the web while passing through an opening, often it was only the candidate for that position who viewed such an occurrence as a failure. Conversely, the group as a whole saw the same event as a learning experience that enabled them to plan better for the next person. Eventually, everyone found a department and was assisted by their colleagues through the Web of Academia without getting stopped by personnel. The following questions were useful in processing the experience in terms of the learning objectives:

1. Who decided which department was right for each person? What information was needed to make that decision? In the office, who decides which person is best suited to work on particular projects and what needs to be known before that decision can be made?
2. When people were stopped by personnel midway in their attempt to pass through the web into a department, how did folks feel (both the candidate and supporting comrades) when personnel declared that we needed a different person for that position? At the office, what does it feel like when a project you initiated is handed over to somebody else? Why would that decision have been made and by whom?
3. If you were withdrawn from a department, was there something you had to offer the group or was your experience wasted? In the office, once someone has taken over a project you got off the ground, is there something that you can offer? Conversely, is there something you would like to receive from colleagues when you hand a project over?

Further than the above issues, dialogue evolved around the issue of offering support versus forcing someone to receive help when verbal encouragement is sufficient. Trust was also a paramount concept discussed.

CONTRIBUTOR

Tim Dixon
Associate Director
Corporate Adventure Training Institute
Brock University
St. Catharines, Ontario
Canada L2S 3A1
(905) 688-5550 ext. 3120

"ERTA"
ESTIMATED RELATIVE TIME ASSESSMENT

INTRODUCTION

This exercise is designed for participants who are new to a group living situation. It can be used with any group provided the individuals can function independently and without direct personal supervision. The goals of the exercise are to provide the individuals with insight into their daily life patterns and to provide support for choosing to consciously change, adapt, and understand choices made each day.

It can be beneficial to provide the opportunity for this exercise to be used both at the beginning and at the end of the residential stay with the intent of the first session reflecting a typical "old" day and the later session to support the "new" day.

SET-UP

A map of the campus site is developed and printed that notes the location of any/all daily activity centers or points. Examples of these would include, but not be limited to, the locations of the kitchen, bathrooms, phones, chapel, sleeping quarters, exercise facilities, business office, lounges, gardens, parking lot, and TV. The group's participants are presented with an individual copy of the map and the framework of the exercise.

It's best to ask that watches not be used. It's also valuable to notify the entire facility staff of the time frame of the exercise to assure that visitations will be acceptable and not disruptive. Consideration should also be given to identifying a way of signalling to all participants the completion of the allotted time.

SAMPLE PRESENTATION

Participants are given the instructions that they must "walk" through one of their own typical days by visiting the appropriate sites on campus that represent their respective daily activities, and do this at a rate reflective of their regular pace. At this point review the map, explaining the representation of sites marked (the chapel may represent time in meditation or contemplation; the parking lot may represent time spent in a car, on a bus, or other means of transportation; the business office may represent school/work). Invite participants to ask questions and/or to identify additional locations and interpretations.

Encourage participants to move from place to place and to pause at each location at a rate reflective of their usual pace and the amount of time they spend at each activity. The exercise is about experiencing the journey and not about finishing the "day" in the allotted time. Participants are given a time frame for the exercise and provided with a scale of converted hours into minutes (such as two minutes equals one hour of "real time"), but this is used as a guideline and should not be used as an evaluation of "success" since timepieces are not required or encouraged.

DEBRIEFING

In discussion, participants are asked to talk about how it felt to move through their daily activities, to share what they liked and didn't like about their "day," to reflect, and, if they are willing, to discuss how they would live their day differently and what they would do to make the changes that they desire. If family living units are a component of the group, consider breaking out into these small groups for part of the discussion.

It is important to include an opportunity to discuss the availability of support for desired change and to consider how one might ask for and identify sources of support in and out of the residential program.

CONTRIBUTOR

Barbara A. "Babs" Baker, MBA
Executive Director
Association for Experiential Education
2885 Aurora Avenue #28
Boulder, CO 80303-2252, USA
(303) 440-8844

MEMBERSHIP RECRUITMENT/ SORORITY RUSH

INTRODUCTION

This frame can be used with sororities, fraternities, or other student organizations that go through a very active membership drive and selection process. This activity may also be particularly helpful when participants will be (or are) living in a common household. Reflection on the recent process of membership status acquisition as well as future issues associated with sharing living space will most likely occur.

GOALS

1. To enhance/increase communication between group members.
2. To increase/introduce significance of cooperation between group members.
3. To identify importance of inclusion/exclusion relative to the group.
4. To familiarize group members with each other.
5. To increase and identify the significance of participation relative to the group's effectiveness and success.

SET-UP

The Star Wars or Diminishing Resources initiative is used for this activity. Facilitators set up this activity by placing numerous roped circles/hula hoops of varying sizes on the ground. The minimum number of circles is the number of participants. Participants are asked to stand in as many groups as there are circles of rope. The facilitator introduces him/herself as the membership rush "guide" (this mirrors the rush process of groups of individuals traveling from house to house). The guide says, "Switch," when (and only when) all participants have successfully placed the soles of both of their feet inside of one of the circles. At that time each group finds a new house or organization to visit if possible. When everyone has found a place and is within the limits of the organization (feet inside the circle), the guide asks each individual to move to a new house/organization. At the same time, facilitators are removing the circles (one by one) until there is only one large circle left for the entire group to be in.

LOGISTICS

Make sure people don't run from circle to circle or fight another participant or facilitator for a circle (or rope). Warn participants to be careful not to trip on ropes. Don't allow participants to piggyback each other in the circle (it is impossible for them to meet the requirement of "feet in" on someone's back!).

DEBRIEFING

Sample questions to group/individuals:

1. How did it feel when houses/organizations began to disappear?
2. Did you think you were going to be able to get everyone into the last house/organization?
3. What did you do in order to get everyone to fit?
4. What were the personal/group consequences for individuals "left out" by the process? How did the group deal with this issue? How will they deal with this issue in the upcoming recruitment process?
5. Were everyone's ideas being heard? If not, how did it feel not to be heard and how as a group can you make sure all voices are acknowledged?
6. What was it like to fit in?
7. As you think about fitting in, what are some ways you can all welcome each other and make each other comfortable in your real house/organization?

CONTRIBUTOR

Adrienne Garrison
1745 Fulmer Street
Ann Arbor, MI 48103, USA

THE PRACTICUM WEB

INTRODUCTION

Students in the Recreation Leaders Program at Arctic College in Inuvik, N.W.T., Canada, do three practicums during the course of their two years of study for a diploma in Recreation. Two of the practicums are six weeks long, while the other one is 12 weeks long. Successful completion of the practicum requires communication and cooperation with a number of groups.

The Spider's Web, described in *Cowstails and Cobras* (Rohnke, 1989), can be used as a metaphor for the practicums. By using the Spider's Web initiative, students can learn the importance of communicating and cooperating with these groups.

GOALS

The main goal is to get students thinking in terms of communication and cooperation with other people.

SET-UP

The Spider's Web is set up in the usual manner. Each student's home community is put on an opening in the web. The three instructors take on the role of: (1) the community, (2) regional/territorial bodies, or (3) college instructors/support. Students who do not yet have practicum placements can take on the role of: (1) interim recreation trainers, (2) community supervisors, or (3) recreation development officers. The students and instructors have to all pass through their opening in the web without touching the web. Successfully getting everyone through the web signifies successfully getting through the practicum.

SAMPLE PRESENTATION

"As students, you will be participating in three practicums. Who are the people you can turn to in order to help you get through your practicums?" The students will list these people and groups. "How can you make it easier to work with these people/groups in order to get through your practicums?" The students will then talk about and list the ways they can work with these people/groups.

LOGISTICS

The solutions to getting through the Spider's Web should come from the students themselves. The instructors are part of the process, but the students have the ability to get through this exercise on their own with little intervention or few ideas from the instructors.

DEBRIEFING

During the debriefing the students can reflect on their experience. Sample questions that could be asked to help group members to learn from the experience and bring out some ideas on how they can get through their practicums are:

1. How did it feel to get through the web?
2. What did you do to make it easier to get through the web?
3. What was the most challenging part about getting through the web?
4. What did you learn by getting the group through this web?
5. Did you learn anything that will help you with your practicums?
6. What did you do to get everybody through the web?

CONTRIBUTOR

Brian Alford
Recreation Leaders Program
Arctic College
P.O. Box 1008
Inuvik, N.W.T.
Canada X0E 0T0

NURTURING FAMILY

INTRODUCTION

For many years, I have taught in programs that begin with a strong classroom base mixed with some direct experiences (usually local field trips). The programs take place over a period of 10 or 11 weeks and are designed to build toward a final expedition. Recently, I have begun to apply this family metaphor as a way to tie together most of the activities we do.

This metaphor has proven to be very helpful in many of the programs that I teach. I know others have used the same idea in other contexts.

GOAL

This metaphor is designed to increase:

1. Levels of interpersonal risk taking.
2. Ability to effectively solve problems in a group.
3. Mutual support.
4. Support for ethical behavior.

SAMPLE PRESENTATION

"Over the years, I have noticed some real differences between groups. Just about every group has a good time and learns a lot, but occasionally a group will go far beyond this and become something that is never forgotten by all of its members. I think what happens is that the group becomes a "family" in the most nurturing sense of the word. What happens is that the members decide to take real risks with each other, just as an ideal family would. Instead of the superficial kind of relationships that we have in most classes, people start to take risks to share real feelings, and not just the angry stuff either, but also the caring stuff.

When conflict arises, as it does in any family, not only is it brought out in the open, but support is offered by the other members of the family. Throughout our time together, you will be faced with new and challenging situations. In our work, and with each other, it makes a a tremendous difference as to what we can achieve as individuals and as a group.

With groups that get to this point, my role stops being that of a traditional authoritative parental figure who 'enforces' the rules, and instead becomes more of an ideal parent who is more of a guide and a participant because other family members take on the responsibilities of being their own parents. When a group becomes a nurturing family, it can be one of the most exciting experiences family members have ever had, because the feeling of mutual support and caring is so strong.

You have a choice. As I said, most groups you are in will never get to this point. It will take a lot of your personal energy and risk-taking to get there. The choice is whether you want just a good learning experience or one that will influence you for a very long time."

CONTRIBUTOR

Tom Lindblade
College of DuPage
Alpha One
Glen Ellyn, IL 60137, USA

CROSSING THE RIVER OF KNOWLEDGE

INTRODUCTION

Crossing the River of Knowledge is designed for any student group that is currently involved in formal education programs working toward a degree. It highlights the idea that as we acquire knowledge we are often moving toward a particular goal (e.g., learning procedures when we start a new job, library research to write a paper, or coursework to obtain a degree). A class of students will often follow similar paths in getting through a degree program and they can support each other in a variety of ways. The River Crossing has a clear-cut objective: Everyone must get across the river to graduate. Supporting each other makes the task easier, and group planning helps to find ways to solve complex problems. This exercise is best done after some ice breakers and one or two other less complex activities.

GOALS

1. To develop support within the group (emotional, content, and physical).
2. To clarify communication and decision-making skills.
3. To examine leadership; how and why leadership may shift during planning and completion of a task.
4. To balance planning with action in solving problems.

SET-UP

This initiative is set up in a typical river crossing arrangement, with four or five 4x4's (which can be moved) and 12 to 15 wooden blocks (which cannot be moved) used to cross the "river." The group is supposed to start at one corner (side) of the river and cross diagonally to the opposite bank. They must start in a 90 degree quadrant formed by the edge of the river and a line perpendicular to the bank of the river extending from the first wooden block. The entire group must cross the river, getting off onto the opposite bank in a similar quadrant extending from the wooden block that is diagonally located at the farthest point from the start block. The fifth 4x4, if utilized, can be placed on a wooden block in a position that is clearly off of the most direct path to the objective, thus signifying a decision to take electives, or acquire knowledge, that is not necessarily required by the degree program.

Safety considerations include: (1) no jumping or running; (2) any movement across the 4x4's is spotted by the facilitator, thus only one person can be moving on the 4x4's at a time (others may stand on the 4x4's, however); (3) warning the group that the 4x4's are prone to turning so they should be cautious when moving across them; and (4) being aware of other people's bodies and heads when lifting and moving the 4x4's.

SAMPLE PRESENTATION

"What you see in front of you is the River of Knowledge, which extends as far as you can see in both directions. You are standing on one bank, secure in the knowledge you have acquired to this point in your educational career. The banks of the river are defined by the wooden blocks, which you can think of as 'pearls of wisdom.' The pearls might be facts you acquire or concepts you learn as you take your coursework. The 4x4's are the bridges or relationships between the pearls of wisdom. Knowledge is not only made up of facts and concepts, but also of the relationships between information. Understanding is learning those relationships. Creativity can be thought of as redefining the relationships or relating ideas and concepts in new and unique ways to answer questions or solve problems.

The quadrant formed by the river bank and a perpendicular line to the bank running from the first pearl of wisdom is a safe and secure area. There is a similar secure area diagonally across the river at the pearl located at the far corner. Your objective is for everyone in your group to reach that secure area. The secure area across the river can be thought of as completing the degree program.

The rest of the river bank area, on this side of the river and on the other side, can be called the 'Swamp of Ignorance.' If anyone steps in these areas at any time, everyone must start again from the beginning. The pearls are safe areas to use as you cross the river, acquiring knowledge as you go. The river is perilous, and should you step into the river, everyone must start again from the beginning.

You have resources available. The 4x4's are bridges, or relationships, between the pearls of wisdom. You can use them to walk or stand on. However, as you know, the river runs fast and deep. Should a 4x4 touch the surface of the river, it will be pulled out of your hands and you will lose it as a resource. Similarly, if a 4x4 should touch the surface of the swamp, it will be pulled from your hands and lost."

At this point, if a fifth 4x4 is being used, the group is told it represents an additional potential resource if they want to decide to go out of their way to get it.

LOGISTICS

Depending on how much difficulty the group is experiencing, "lost" 4x4 resources can be placed on one of the out-of- the-way pearls so the group can recover them if they really need to do so.

Model and point out positive feedback for the group as individuals make progress.

DEBRIEFING

Debrief the kinds of support people provided to each other. The physical support in this activity may be obvious. Students often help each other with emotional support as they progress through a degree program, as well as providing informational or content support that assists individuals in making choices.

Communication characteristics can be thoroughly debriefed. Maintaining good communication with each other, with faculty, and with academic advisors is important. It is particularly useful to spend time discussing listening skills. If the opportunity is present, blend decision-making into this portion of the discussion as well.

The River Crossing is a complex, multifaceted activity that can be made more or less difficult depending upon the group. Many other topics can be debriefed depending upon the issues that emerge from the experience.

CONTRIBUTOR

Ronald C. Comer, PhD
Ohio State University, College of Medicine
Office of Academic Services
076 Health Sciences Library
376 W. 10th Avenue
Columbus, Ohio 43210, USA
(614) 292-6192

THE TENSION TRAVERSE AS A METAPHOR FOR PROBLEMATIC GROUP DYNAMICS IN INIDIVIDUAL TEAM SPORTS AT THE COLLEGE LEVEL

INTRODUCTION

The Tension Traverse initiative can be used effectively to address problematic group dynamics in individual team sports at the college level. Individual team sports can include wrestling, gymnastics, swimming and diving, golf, etc., where an individual team member competes against an opponent, one on one, and that individual's score, win or lose, contributes to the overall team outcome. Additionally, with these particular sports, there is varying intra-team competition in terms of limited spots available for individuals for particular meets or matches; team members compete against other team members in order to secure a spot. This can lead to problematic intra-team dynamics.

GOALS

This initiative can emphasize:

1. The reduction of intra-team competitiveness by channeling awareness and energy of individuals towards increased team support through cooperation.
2. Improved communication among members of the team, including coaches, athletes, and support staff.
3. Enhanced compassion through team members recognizing each individual's strengths and weaknesses, contributions, and worth.

SET-UP

The set-up for the initiative is the typical Tension Traverse. It consists of a length of cable tautly stretched and connected between six to eight trees, on somewhat varying terrain, approximately 18" above the ground. Distance between trees can vary, but should be far enough to present some challenge to the group.

SAMPLE PRESENTATION

Before the entire group, the facilitator states, "Here is a cable stretched between a number of trees. This cable represents a meet in which your team is about to compete. You are all standing at the first tree, the beginning of the meet; at the far end of the cable the last tree represents the end of the meet. In between the trees is a series of cables representing the various individual matches or events in the meet. The object for all of you is to get the entire team from the first tree to the last tree, crossing each section of cable without touching the ground. If any individual falls off the cable and touches the ground at any time, the entire team must to go back to the first tree and begin the meet again. Each of you has individual strengths, skills, and talents that you utilize in your own individual match; yet in order to succeed as a team, you'll need to cooperate and work together in your meet."

There may be certain instances where a team becomes heavily dependent upon one, two, or three individuals who seem to "carry" the team. If this is the case, an interesting twist on the Tension Traverse initiative is to "handicap" these individuals through the use of a blindfold, loosely securing one arm to the body, or restricting their verbal communication.

LOGISTICS

As a facilitator, I choose to remain out of the activity in order to observe the individuals and team in their problem-solving, cooperation, and communication. With the low height of the cable, safety is not of great concern, providing the ground surface is clear of debris and fairly soft (a forest floor of leaves and duff with fallen limbs and branches removed is ideal). Additionally, it's sometimes helpful to explain to the participants that if they feel they are starting to fall off the cable, let go right away, step off for a safe landing, and not to try to remain on the cable "at all costs." It may be necessary to provide some spotting support for the individuals in the initiative.

DEBRIEFING

The debrief should focus back on the goals of the initiative activity. Questions which could be addressed to individuals and the team might include:

1. What seemed to help your team succeed in this meet?
2. Did anything hinder or get in the way of your individual/ team effort?
3. What roles did individual team members play in this meet?
4. What was the "high point/low point" for you as an individual team member in this meet?
5. How did you as a team member individually feel about this meet?
6. What did you learn, both individually and as a team, about a meet?

CONTRIBUTOR

Steve W. Burr, PhD
Western Illinois University
Department of Recreation, Parks, and Tourism Administration
400 Currens Hall
Macomb, IL 61455, USA
(309) 298-1967

ROPE LOOPS
AS A METAPHOR FOR CHANGE

INTRODUCTION

This activity works well as an introductory initiative. The size of the group may vary from 6 to 20 people. The group must be willing work together to push their "comfort zones" to be successful.

GOALS

The goal of this initiative is for all group members to share resources, to work together, and to feel more comfortable around each other by gradually expanding their comfort zones.

SET-UP

The set-up for this activity is the same as the standard Star Wars activity. Several ropes tied in circle loops are needed for this activity. The loops should be one to three feet in diameter (the lengths of the ropes can vary). Cut-up retired climbing ropes or jump ropes work well. Each rope needs to be large enough for at least one person's feet to fit completely within the loop. I start with as many loops as there are participants. To start the activity, have the participants stand in a large circle.

SAMPLE PRESENTATION

"For this next activity, I will be giving each of you a rope loop. Once you have a loop, please place it on the ground/floor and stand in it (wait for participants to do this). In life, we all have our own opinions and perspectives. A lot can be gained, though, from taking the time to find out what other people think. As a staff, you work together closely and are constantly discovering not only new things about yourself but also others. What are some changes that you or the group may experience? (Let the group provide responses.)

"The time you will be spending together here can be a time of growth and change for every member of the group. The rope loops that you are standing in are meant to represent change. The only rule for this activity is that your feet must be entirely contained within a loop. Every time that I say "change" you have to give up a loop. You as a group may choose which loop you would like to give up. If I see someone with their feet outside of the loop or the air space above it, I will ask that person to adapt to the change. Are there any questions?"

LOGISTICS

As the facilitator, you should be an observer during this activity. Make sure that all participants keep their feet within the loops or the space above them. Once you have determined that everyone is following the one rule of the activity, call out "change." Continue to do this as long as participants are finding new ways to include everybody. If the group is having problems, encourage them to try to think of new ways to solve the problem. It is important that the facilitator give positive support to the group. Congratulate the group for successes, whether small or large.

DEBRIEFING

The group may figure out that sitting down is one of the only ways to fit everyone into one loop. If they do, ask them: "What were some of the different things that you tried? What kept you from sitting down sooner? How is this like real life? What are some examples? Remind them that success can often be self-determined and of the number of times they were successful.

CONTRIBUTOR

Tracie Van Gheem
Intern, Center for Leadership Development
St. Norbert College
De Pere, WI 54115-2099, USA

MOTIVATION TAG AS A METAPHOR FOR GIVING AND RECEIVING POSITIVE AFFIRMATIONS

INTRODUCTION

This activity works well as a group exercise in giving and receiving positive affirmations. Motivation Tag should be used with a group that knows each other or is beginning to know one another fairly well. Safety hazards can be prevented be enforcing a "walking only" rule and setting clear boundaries.

GOALS

Motivation Tag emphasizes the importance of positive self-talk and helps participants to practice giving and receiving affirmations. This activity focuses on personal growth and encourages individuals to accept compliments to improve their own self-images. Motivation Tag also enables participants to use teamwork as a method of overcoming sarcasm, devaluation, and negative self-talk.

SET-UP

The facilitator should set up specific boundaries for this activity, such as rope or cones. Colored bandannas, flags, or some other material can indicate the individuals who are "it."

SAMPLE PRESENTATION

Begin briefing Motivation Tag by asking participants the following question: "Have any of you ever heard of the term 'positive affirmation'?" If their answer is yes, ask someone in the group to briefly explain the term. If their answer is no, explain that positive affirmation is a way to elevate the self-esteem of yourself or others by positively affirming your/their strength, (e.g., a compliment). "This activity is called Motivation Tag and it will give you the opportunity to practice giving and receiving positive affirmations. Before I explain the rules, please form a circle.

I would like each of you to take a look around this circle and think for a moment about the strengths of your fellow group members. Try to think of one or two positive affirmations (compliments) that you could give to each person in this group. You don't need to say them aloud, but try to remember them because you will need to recall these affirmations during the activity." (Pause for one to two minutes to let participants think of these affirmations.)

"We will begin by assigning two people to be 'it.' If you are tagged by someone who is 'it,' you are frozen, and must stand still until someone thaws you. If someone becomes frozen, it is the job of everyone who is not 'it' to help (thaw) that person. The goal of the 'its' is to tag all of the other participants before they can become thawed.

The thawing process has three important parts. They are: (1) the frozen person must be tagged; (2) tagging person has five seconds of free time to verbally give the frozen person positive affirmation (example: 'Mary, you are very intelligent!' Superficial compliments, such as 'Mary, your hair looks nice today' do not count. The affirmation should relate only to non-physical attributes); and (3) the frozen person must verbally repeat the affirmation (example: 'I am very intelligent!') to become completely thawed. After repeating it, that person may leave his or her spot. As soon as an 'it' person becomes tired, that person should announce that he or she will need someone else to take his or her place. The 'it' people will carry these markers (show the group the bandannas, flags, etc.). The boundaries for the activity are . . . (safe boundaries). Please remember to be careful when walking and tagging. Who would like to be 'it' first?" Give these two or three persons (depending on group size) the bandannas or flags.

LOGISTICS

The facilitator should either take on an interested observer role in this activity or volunteer to be "it" for the first round. Facilitators should not actively participate because participants may feel uncomfortable giving affirmations to a facilitator whom they might not know very well. As an observer, the facilitator has the opportunity to gather valuable processing information related to the types of affirmations being given and to the relative difficulty that participants are experiencing in giving and accepting affirmations.

DEBRIEFING

This activity should take approximately 10–15 minutes. Debriefing questions for Motivation Tag may include the following: "Was it easier to give or to receive affirmations? How did you feel when you had to repeat the affirmations? How often do you normally give and receive compliments?"

CONTRIBUTOR

Lisa K. Fels
Intern, Center for Leadership Development
St. Norbert College
De Pere, WI 54115-2099, USA

THE COMMUNICATION WEB: ACTIVE LISTENING SKILLS

INTRODUCTION

The communication skills concerning active listening can often be explored and experienced through the low ropes element called the Spider's Web (Rohnke, 1989). The objective in this activity is to pass each individual through a fabricated web without touching any strands of the web. Once a member of the group passes through a web opening, it closes indefinitely or temporarily for passage by another individual. The opening and closing of the web passageways are dictated by whether or not any member of the group touches any part of the web. The theme of this set-up of the Spider's Web initiative concerns positive listening skills and poor listening behaviors.

GOALS

The emphasis of this activity is to increase students' awareness and practice of active listening skills, which may include:

1. Maintaining eye contact between the speaker and listener.
2. Allowing the speaker to talk without interruptions.
3. Extending non-verbal listening cues.
4. Staying focused on the speaker.
5. Asking questions related to the present conversation.
6. Paraphrasing the speaker's thoughts.
7. Not reacting to and judging the thoughts of the speaker.

SET-UP

Initiating this activity requires rope and/or twine that can be fabricated into the form of a Spider's Web. Refer to *Cowstails and Cobras II* (Rohnke, 1989) for the traditional set-up rules and design ideas, or *The Bottomless Bag* (Rohnke, 1988) for a materials list and fabrication specifications for a portable Spider's Web. Also include a roll of masking tape to be used to close off web passageways. Enough passageways, plus several extra, must be incorporated into the web to accommodate each individual in the group. The complexity and difficulty (sizes and shapes) of the web should be determined based on the physical ability and developmental readiness of the group. The recommended group size ranges from eight to 12 people. Consequently, the group size will not be too large to negate the emphasis on engaging in active listening skills and the group will not be too small to complete the activity with minimal challenge.

Prior to presenting the activity and developing the metaphor, have the students brainstorm indicators that show someone is actively listening to them when they speak. Conversely, ask the group to present behaviors that indicate that they are not being listened to while talking. This brainstorming can be done as a group or in the form of dyad/triad sharing. In this sharing, each person comments on the question for one and one-half minutes while the others actively listen. Immediately at the end of this time, the focus switches to the next person to speak in the dyad/triad. After this process has been completed, the entire group congregates and a representative from each dyad/triad presents several of the thoughts pertinent to the subject.

SAMPLE PRESENTATION

"Each time we meet an unfamiliar person or communicate with someone we already know, the lines of communication move along a continuum from being completely closed to completely opened. With acquaintances, communication may start off at a superficial level. With other people in our lives, such as friends, teachers, siblings, and parents, lines of communication open and close based on the feelings of trust, respect, and safety. Many of these feelings are directly tied into whether or not you feel you are being heard. In this web of communication, the few passageways that are closed (with masking tape) indicate the paths of communication that are not open in a relationship for whatever reason. The strands of the web are sticky and fragile, sometimes resulting in your breaking them without being aware. This can occur when you are unable to perceive that you are not listening to another person. As each of you passes through this web, without adversely affecting a line of communication by not touching any part of the web, then one of the passageways to good communication opens (remove the tape from one section). If anyone touches a line of the web while one person in the group is being passed through the web, then that passageway to good communication becomes closed (apply masking tape). The person being passed through the web during this breakdown in communication must return to attempt to reestablish communication by being passed through another passageway. Remember that lines of communication are fragile and can be broken easily and are sometimes difficult to reestablish and open."

DEBRIEFING

During the debrief, return to the indicators that show someone is listening to you and the behaviors that indicate you are not being heard. At this point, the students can point out which ones they exhibited during the activity. The following are several of the many questions that can be asked:

1. Do people shut off lines of communication with you without their being aware?
2. How do you let people know that you are not feeling heard?
3. Is a broken line of communication easy or difficult to repair? Why?
4. What things will you communicate with anyone? With no one?
5. Why and how does fear prevent you from communicating feelings, thoughts, and ideas?

CONTRIBUTOR

Andy Greif
RR 1, Box 3082
Kennebunk, ME 04043, USA
(207) 985-3727

MOON BALL
AS A METAPHOR FOR GOAL SETTING

INTRODUCTION

The Moon Ball activity can be a great team builder. I feel that the key to this activity is in how the facilitator explains it. This activity can be used with almost any group.

GOALS

The goal of this activity is for the group to work together as a team. In the process, they can learn more about themselves and each other. The metaphors of goal setting and leadership can tie in well with this activity.

SET-UP

All you will need for this activity is a beach ball and an area large enough for the ball to be hit around. This activity can be done inside or outside.

SAMPLE PRESENTATION

"This activity is called Moon Ball. Before the activity, I'd like everyone to take some time and think about a goal that you have. The goal can be something small or big, something in the near future or far off. In a minute, we'll go around the circle and have a chance to share our goals of the group." (Facilitators may wish to wait and think of their own goal so they can also share it with the group.)

Go around the circle and listen to everyone's goals. "These all sound like great goals! For this activity, Moon Ball, the goal is to keep the ball in the air without letting it hit the ground. How many times do you think that we can hit this ball and keep it in the air?" (Facilitator: Wait for the group to come to a decision.) "What are some things that we can do to reach our goal? (Listen to these and ask the group to consider these in accomplishing the task.) Okay, let's start."

LOGISTICS

This activity can work well whether the facilitator participates or not. It may help the group to get to know the facilitator better by being informal with the group during this activity. As the activity progresses, let different members in the group take on leadership roles. One of the best things about this activity is that it can give everyone the opportunity to be both a leader and a follower. During the activity, continue to encourage the group. Stop them from time to time if they are having problems and ask them if anyone has any ideas that can help the group to reach their goal. Reinforce the group to support other members and be positive. Observe leadership in the participants.

DEBRIEFING

This activity may take the group a long time to achieve if they have set a high goal. Recently, I ran a group of nine high school students that set a goal of 100. They readjusted their goal to 30 with the hope of moving on to 100 after they were successful at a smaller number. We were out in the wind and it was challenging. We could not get past 19 hits. The group began to get down on themselves and each other. A good question to ask if this happens is "How would you like to be treated if you missed the ball?" or "What are some ways that we can support each other?" If the group does not reach their goal, questions that could be asked include: "What were some of the different things that you tried? What was the highest number that we reached? What could we have done differently? Would you like to try the activity again or move on? How is this like real life? What are some examples of things that keep people from reaching their goals?"

The high school students I was working with wanted to keep going. Finally we reached the small goal of 30 and continued to 136. Not only was I impressed, but they were too! They ranked it as their favorite activity of the day. If the group does reach its goal, you could ask them: "What were some of the different things that you tried? What finally allowed us to reach our goal? What are some things each of you can do to reach your goals in life?" To focus on leadership, ask the group questions like "What leadership characteristics did you see different people demonstrate?" and "How did this leadership help the group?"

CONTRIBUTOR:

Tracie Van Gheem
Center for Leadership Development
St. Norbert College
De Pere, WI 54115-2099, USA

GENERAL POPULATIONS

CONTEMPLATION EXERCISES FOR ACTIVE, CREATIVE THINKING

INTRODUCTION

Making metaphoric connections by using adventure activities and participatory parables can be a saintly way to teach. Great teachers, such as Christ, Mohammed, and Socrates, used story, action, and metaphor as a non-ego threatening way to guide students to active, creative thinking. Nature also provides another invaluable method of metaphorical teaching. However, in many instances, men and women have placed themselves above nature and removed themselves from their daily interactions with nature. This is tragic, for we are all metaphorically attached, both living and non-living things. Denying that we are a part of nature strips us of a valuable and powerful guidance tool.

This denial, which is our own creation, is of enormous magnitude. The questions we ask exclusively of our own species, and thus the answers we get, are limited in scope with an extremely narrow outlook of one perspective among millions of perspectives. Our tendency to "cheer for the home human team" has led to human arrogance. This arrogance has created blinders to creative solutions and sometimes led us to depend on counselors, many of whom are isolated themselves from a relationship with the natural world. Instead, these professionals sometimes are tied to the industrial world, its paperwork, and the $100/ hour fee.

Each person can benefit from constructing his/her own metaphoric connections to the vast pool of knowledge accessible to all by observing, questioning, tolerating, listening to, and learning from nature. Nature is a huge reservoir of cultures (anything in creation is a culture). With practice, each person can develop his/her own unique tool for guidance to applicable answers to personal, unique situations. No teacher/student rebellions, no $100 fee, no false sense of superiority. Individuals need to practice contemplation regularly to develop this extremely valuable tool.

Before sending individuals out to find their own contemplation spots, you might give them one of the following examples to familiarize them with the process you are trying to have them practice.

SAMPLE PRESENTATION

Introduce this activity to a group by giving them an example of how we are like every other living thing. Use one of these contemplation suggestions to make your point and/or read an example from one of Tom Brown's *Tracker* books. You may ask the group to focus on the same subject for contemplation or have them pick a focus of their own.

SUGGESTION #1

Contemplate the following questions alone for a half hour while walking through woods. How does the way trees grow suggest that trees and we are cousins?

Have each individual walk through the forest with a variety of terrain. Each is to contemplate how the trees grow and attempt to see some linkage between treeism and humanism. There are sure to be multiple right answers. Encourage and accept them all. I often say, "Have you ever noticed that trees growing on a steep slope tend to grow straighter than those that grow in a flat part of the forest?"

CONCLUSION

Those in the flat part of the forest have to complete more for life-giving sunlight than the ones growing on a hillside where all the trees can easily get all the sunlight they require. Have you ever noticed that when parents go to see their young children perform in their first theatrical production they struggle to get a good view of their soon-to-be Academy Award winners? They strain every muscle fiber to see around or get above those in front of them because elementary schools don't generally have it in their budget to afford elevated viewing seats. Now they might be able to sit up straight if the same production was held in a theatre with elevated seats. Does this remind you of the same struggle in the tree family?

SUGGESTION #2

This suggestion works well with a group that has all different degrees of fire-lighting skills.

Contemplate the word and the phenomenon "fire."

Think about fire.

Why would you want to make a fire if you don't have the conveniences of the modern home?

How would you go about making a fire with a friend, a family member, a lover (we're not talking about a sexual fire but a relationship one)?

What can the process of firebuilding teach us about our relationships to other people? What makes a successful fire? What makes a meaningful relationship?

CONCLUSION

We are sitting by a stream on a sunny day. From our Sun—the ultimate fire—comes all life, and without it there would be no life here on Earth. Fire is passion-love. The Sun is the number-one lover. From the water that flows by me and the Sun that shines down on me comes the "savings account" of love/fire—trees that in one form or another will sustain me in body and spirit. Were I not in modern society with electricity and stoves and central heating, I would have to depend a great deal on fire to warm me, cook my food, and to provide light to draw other humans to me. I would have to draw on the savings account that the Sun has provided for me (i.e., wood to make fire).

A good fire depends on the fuel you use. It can be thick or skinny, hard or soft, wet or dry, from the ground or off a tree, with pitch pockets or without. A good fire depends on where you build it, with whom you build it (e.g., do they help or hinder the building and life of the fire?), how you arrange the fuel, where you hold the match, and whether you've gathered enough and the right kind of fuel for your purpose. Patience and faith are necessary. Poking and prodding can upset and kill a fire and a relationship. Tinder (i.e., a small amount of commitment to a task or relationship) alone will burn fast and the relationship (the fire) needs constant attention and takes away from its purpose (e.g., cooking, warmth, ambiance, gratification, appreciation). A good fire needs a good starter (tinder), patience, understanding, and good hardwood fuel logs (e.g., the greater the commitment the better the chances for a worthy fire or relationship or a task well done). Good fuel logs (high commitment) will ensure a hot fire (a functioning relationship) that suits the purpose for which it was intended. When the gatherers of firewood have gathered enough good wood to satisfy the needs of their fire (the intended purpose), they can stop running for fuel and appreciate what they have done together. Helpers, lovers, parents, and children can appreciate the memories of their well-conceived, planned, and executed fire (love). And as the coals and embers die away, with love and warmth so do its builders. When the rain falls the remaining ash (our dead bodies) is washed into the earth, where the earth, sun, and water, in a relationship eons old, cooperate to reinvest in the bank account of fire (love). This bank account is full of trees. The cycle then repeats itself.

DEBRIEFING

The process of seeing ourselves (humans) as a part of nature and nature as our most skilled, polite, loving teacher will take a high degree of commitment, trust, patience, and practice. It took us all quite a while to learn our multiplication tables. It will probably take some time for us to reopen the links of communication with nature which we have viewed so long as subservient to us.

As a part of your communication practice, try spending a half hour each day (a cooking timer with an alarm is good—you don't want to let the old wristwatch grab your attention too much) in a quiet communicative place with nature. Bring a journal and pen with you. Breathe deeply and in the first few minutes select a word that comes to you, e.g., *green, breeze, sound, light, stone, stream*. Sit quietly where you are. Focus your mind gently on the word you have chosen and when a thought comes into your head associated with your word, hang on to it. When an unassociated thought comes in, gently bring the focus of your thought back to your chosen word. Let the communications of nature form around your word. After your timer goes off, record as briefly or extensively as you like the essence of your communication between you and the cosmos.

CONTRIBUTOR

John Dyett
Thomas Road, RFD 1 #315
Greenfield, NH 03047, USA
(603) 547-2180

VISITING A SENIORS' HOME

This metaphor is for building relationships, enhancing self-esteem, making life choices, and grieving loss.

INTRODUCTION

This activity has been used successfully with a wide variety of groups, including substance abusers, family members, and professionals. It can involve emotional risk-taking, often depending on the participant's willingness to interface with the residents of the seniors' home and to process their feelings.

GOAL

This activity emphasizes: (1) building partnerships with older, non-threatening adults; (2) experiencing the joy and increase in self-esteem as a result of bringing youthful energy and caring into the lives of seniors; (3) getting in touch with the grief around the loss of significant family members, especially grandparents and parents; (4) becoming aware of one's mortality; (5) reflecting on choices one makes during their time on earth; and (6) taking stock of what we do have in terms of our health, how to keep it, and how to use one's health to create a satisfying life.

SET-UP

The set-up for this activity is to brief participants prior to arriving at the seniors' home as to the goals for the day (see above) and the possibility of intense emotions, especially sadness, grief, and loss. Encourage participants to seek out staff and/or take a break (leaving the room, going outside) as they feel the need.

On arriving at the seniors' home, I ask one of the participants to read the Residents' Bill of Rights (see Attachment 1). This is followed by a 30–45 minute service project (e.g., raking leaves, washing windows), if available. Then, to break the ice I schedule a 15–30-minute getting acquainted time around coffee and donuts with participants talking to residents. Moving into the activities for the day, I have found that two 45-minute activities with a break in between works well for both residents and participants. An exercise class guided by a physical or movement therapist and a percussion jam session are two activities that can engage everyone. The exercise class gives participants insight about the realities of the body as one gets older, while the jam session allows participants to bring some joy and energy into the lives of seniors. Lunch occurs separately. This gives the seniors a break from the participants, and the participants a break from the seniors. It's also a time for participants to debrief around issues/feelings that may have arisen thus far. After lunch, I have participants interview the seniors, usually two to three participants per senior, using the questions in Attachment 2 as a guide. I follow this with another debrief in which participants report back the findings of their interview. Below is a sample schedule.

SAMPLE SCHEDULE

8:45   Arrive Seniors' Home/Read Residents' Bill of Rights
8:55   Service project
9:30   Coffee and donuts with residents
10:00   Exercise class with residents
10:45   Juice/milk break (residents served by participants)
11:00   Music jam session with residents
12:00   Lunch
12:30   Process group around mornings activities
1:00   Participants interview residents
1:30   Process group around interviews
2:15   Leave Seniors' Home

DEBRIEFING

The debriefing usually focuses on: the fear around the reality of becoming old, the gratefulness for being young and healthy and having the opportunity to create one's life or turn one's life around, the increase in self-esteem associated with bringing joy into another's life, the sense of loss and sadness around the loss of a parent and/or grandparent. For younger participants in a recovery setting, these losses may be of someone who was looked upon as an advocate.

ATTACHMENT #1
RESIDENTS' BILL OF RIGHTS

I am a resident of a seniors' home.

I am a human being who, through my contributions to society during my productive years helped to mold a decent place to live for my generation and the generations that followed me. I deserve to be treated with respect and dignity just as I have always tried to treat others. I am and have been "Somebody" over the years, to many people, such as:

My Sweetheart—My Wife—My Husband

My Mother—My Father

My Daughter—My Son

My Many Friends

If the waning years have been unkind to me—I don't see well, I don't hear well, I spill my food, I am incontinent, I need help often, I am cranky (though I don't want to be)— please don't blame me.

I could be your Mother— Father

Grandmother—Grandfather

Someday you may be a "Me." A little kindness, a soft word, some acknowledgement by you that I am still a person, not a "thing," is all I ask.

ATTACHMENT #2
SENIORS' HOME INTERVIEW

Hi! My name is_____ and I'm from_____ . I would like to ask you a few questions about your life.

1. *Do you see yourself as having lived a full life?*
2. *What is success?*
3. *What was a big challenge in your life? How did you meet that challenge?*

4. *What is/was the most difficult part of your life emotionally?*
5. *When you were having the most fun in your life, what were you doing?*
6. *Who is/was the most important person in your life?*
7. *What are you looking forward to?*
8. *If you had a chance to live your life over, what would you do differently, if anything?*
9. *What is the key to getting along with other people?*

CONTRIBUTOR

Rudy Pucel
59 Woodbury Street
Keene, NH 03431, USA
(603) 357-7232

THE CHOCOLATE GAME

INTRODUCTION

This works best with a group of people who are together for an extended period of time (several days at least). It is designed to identify competitive and cooperative behaviors and how these behaviors may change over time and situation. It is ideal for those groups that have been "therapied out" and think they know all the correct responses. The most appropriate setting is around the campfire or stove after supper. There is often uncooperative behavior, so be prepared!

GOALS

The goal of this activity is to demonstrate that cooperative behavior pays off in the long run. However, isolated competitive (selfish) behavior in this activity can produce desirable results for individuals, but often at the expense of the remaining group members and the total community.

SET-UP

The supplies needed are:

    a. Two sets of sequentially numbered poker chips (one blue set and one red set).

    b. Two small stuff sacks labelled "CHOICE" and NON-CHOICE.

    c. A sufficient supply of M&Ms.

    d. A set of "pay-out matrices" (one for each participant and instructor).

The group sits in a circle and the rules are explained carefully. Make sure everyone understands, and answer any questions. Be careful not to offer judgements about the worth of cooperation versus competition. Also make sure to provide each participant with a copy of the "pay-out matrix" (see page 229).

The group is then permitted to discuss strategy. It must be emphasized that all decisions and actions are personal and secret. Once each person has made his/her choice, one chip is placed in the CHOICE bag and the other is placed in the NON-CHOICE bag.

Each individual is identified by the number on the poker chip. The M&Ms must be secretly distributed according to the pay-out matrix.

SAMPLE PRESENTATION

A group of eight participants: Maria = #1, George = #2, Jose = #3, Pierre = #4, Louise = #5, Zak = #6, Deb = #7, and Jodi = #8. The names and numbers are pre-recorded and the chips are distributed accordingly. Sit the students around the fire after a supper where no dessert has been served. This activity will count as dessert each day, thus creating a "craving" for chocolate. Distribute the pay-out matrix to each participant. Now read the following instructions:

INSTRUCTIONS

Read these instructions to the participants when they have the pay-out matrix in front of them and they each have a red and a blue numbered poker chip:

> The matrix in front of you indicates how you may earn some M&Ms. As a group you may spend as long as you wish discussing the problem and coming up with a decision as to what color chip to choose and what color chip not to choose.
>
> The pay-out matrix will give you the various payouts according to the combination of choices made by the group.
>
> Even though the discussion in your group may reach a decision or consensus, you are still at liberty to make your own choice. Your choice is secret and the payout is secret.
>
> Once the entire group is happy and you have made up your mind, put the CHOICE in your right hand and your NON-CHOICE in your left hand. I will then come around to each individual and you may place your chips in the appropriate bag without anyone else observing your choice.
>
> Only I will know who made what choice and I will distribute the M&Ms discretely. By the number of M&Ms you receive,

you will be able to determine the kinds of choices your friends made but you will not be able to identify who made what choice.

Following the deliberations, when the group comes to a consensus that they should all choose red because it yields the maximum payoff for the group, each participant makes his or her final decision. The facilitator goes around the group and each person puts his/her choices in the appropriate bags without anyone else seeing the color of the chips.

The facilitator observes that in the CHOICE bag there is one blue chip (#4) and the remainder are red. According to the pay-out matrix all participants will receive four M&Ms except for Pierre who will receive 10 M&Ms. No one is expected to reveal how many M&Ms he/she receives. However, when Louise sees that she only received four M&Ms she knows (from the payout matrix) that one person cheated and put in a blue chip. Of course, no one need ever know who was uncooperative.

The next day the entire activity is repeated and the group both decides and promises to make the same choice of red. However, three participants, Pierre (who received 10 yesterday), Jose, and Deb feel they have convinced everyone to cooperate, but independently they intend to put in a blue chip. The result now is that there are three blue chips in the CHOICE bag. According to the pay-out matrix, Pierre, Jose, and Deb each receive six M&Ms. The remainder of the group only receive two each. It soon becomes clear that by cheating you can receive many M&Ms but at the expense of everyone else. The maximum payoff occurs when ALL participants choose red.

LOGISTICS

There are a few pre-conditions which help to accentuate the metaphor. They are:

1. Try to make sure that the participants really crave chocolate or something sweet. This occurs best immediately after supper when there is no dessert available, and is better still if no sugar has been served throughout the day.
2. For maximum effect, the activity should be conducted at least once per day for several days. It is not long before the participants start asking to play the chocolate game because they really want some chocolate. This merely enhances the possibil-

ity of someone being uncooperative and adds power to the metaphor.

3. It is much easier for the facilitator if the same numbers are assigned to a specific participant each time.

4. It is important to be strict with the distribution of the M&Ms. When the activity is over, put the remaining M&Ms somewhere safe. Do not give out "extras" because it undermines the activity.

DEBRIEFING

It soon becomes obvious that to achieve the maximum payout each person must put in a red chip. It also is apparent how many people cheated when the participants count up their own payout. When it is realized that one or two people cheated, the feeling of the group may be one of being let down, especially when everyone agreed to be cooperative ahead of time. The fact that the cheater can remain anonymous makes it even worse. As the sessions progress, the degree of cooperation may ebb and flow. Ultimately the results level out at a point where everyone is willing to make a red choice because that is the only way to enjoy the maximum payout.

Note: There was one case where a group of young offenders played this game for several days and one individual was skillfull enough to con everyone into putting in a red chip and she put in a blue chip. This meant that she always received many more M&Ms, but used them during the day to buy favors such as the carrying of her pack and doing her chores and duties.

CONTRIBUTOR

Dr. Anthony Richards
Youth Research Unit
Division of Leisure Studies
Dalhousie University
6230 South Street
Halifax, Nova Scotia
Canada B3H 3J5

PAY-OUT MATRIX

RED CHOICE		BLUE CHOICE		GROUP
How Many People	How Many M&Ms	How Many people	How Many M&Ms	How Many M&Ms
8	5	0	–	40
7	4	1	10	38
6	3	2	8	34
5	2	3	6	28
4	1	4	4	20
3	0	5	2	10
2	0	6	0	0
1	0	7	0	0

A new matrix will have to be devised for each group size. Make sure that the total payout when all participants cooperate is the maximum.

LIST OF ACTIVITIES

Acid River/Meuse   91, 135, 198

Balance Broom   75, 103
Beam   85
Blind Square/Polygon   41, 142
Blind Toss
Blind Walk   35, 55, 60
Blob Tag   84–85

Chocolate Game   225

Diminishing Resources/Star Wars
Disclosure Activities   113
Disk Jockeys   79

Egg Drop   32
Egg Stand   130

Group Termination   101

Here to There   50–52, 180–181
High Ropes Activities   155–158, 167
Hiking
Hog Call   27–31

Maze
Minefield   82–83
Mineshaft   145–147
Mohawk Walk/Traverse   49, 67
Moon Ball   69–70, 212
Meuse   (See Acid River/Meuse)

Nitro Crossing
Nuclear/Toxic Waste (or Three Mile Island)   53–54, 151–153, 159–160, 184–186

Orienteering/Map work   84–86

Pamper Pole   63
Personal Disclosure Activities

Rebirth Tire   58
Reflection Exercises   217–220
River Crossing (see Acid River/Meuse)
Rock Climbing   118–122
Rope Ladder   167–169

Senior Home Visits   221
Service Projects
Smaug's Jewels   71
Spider's Web   124, 139, 182, 187, 194, 209
Stand Off   38–40
Star Wars   192–204

Tag Games   206–208
Tension Traverse   201–203
Trolleys   88, 175
Trust Fall   52–53
Trust Lifts   98–100

Wall   63, 64–66, 106–108, 109–111
Wall Traverse   61–62
Wild Woosey   44–47, 56–57, 96–97
White Water Kayaking   126

LIST OF CONTRIBUTORS

Alford, Brian   194

Baker, Barbara   191

Barrett, Steph   129

Bartel, Paula   131

Baumgartner, Mark   78

Burr, Steve   203

Cain, Jim   163, 166

Chernov, Richard   186

Comer, Ronald   200

Curtis, Anthony   48

Davis, Bob   105

DiBenedetto, Andrea   66, 83

Dixon, Tim   189

Dyett, John   220

Errico, Philip   81

Fels, Lisa   208

Foster, John   144

Timothy, Francis   100

Gass, Michael   31, 154

Gassner, Greg   68, 70

Garrison, Adrienne   193

Gerstein, Jackie   34

Gillis, Lee   125

Graham, Scott   112

Greif, Andy   66, 83, 117, 211

Groff, Diane   102

Hearn, Betsy   37

Itin, Christian   43, 108

Lair, Michael   138

Lindblade, Tom   197

Lique-Naitove, Peter   95, 97

Lynch, Juli   63

MacLeod, Jay   74

Mathias, Nancy   183

Meyers, Daniel J.   123

Moore, Jim   40

Orr, Jo Ann   40

Piranian, Deb   181

Priest, Simon   147, 150, 154, 158

Richards, Anthony   228

Rieske, Robin   90

Ritchie, Phil   68, 70

Pucel, Rudy   224

Rosenberg, Howard   172

Rubendall, Rob   160

Santucci, Michele   179

Spiller, Simon   141

Trojan, Shelly   131

Van Gheem, Tracie   205, 214

Vorsteg, Anna Kay   31

Welsh, Brian   179

White, Noland   74

Williams, Bobbie   170

BOOKS BY KARL ROHNKE

The Bottomless Bag. (1988). Dubuque, IA: Kendall/Hunt Publishing Co., in partnership with Project Adventure.

The Bottomless Baggie. (1991). Dubuque, IA: Kendall/Hunt Publishing Co., in partnership with Project Adventure.

Cowstails and Cobras. (1989). Dubuque, IA: Kendall/Hunt Publishing Co., in partnership with Project Adventure.

Silver Bullets. (1984). Dubuque, IA: Kendall/Hunt Publishing Co., in partnership with Project Adventure.

ADDITIONAL BOOKS FROM THE ASSOCIATION FOR EXPERIENTIAL EDUCATION PUBLISHED BY KENDALL/HUNT

THE THEORY OF EXPERIENTIAL EDUCATION, THIRD EDITION

Karen Warren, Mitchell Sakofs, and Jasper S. Hunt, Jr., editors
ISBN #0-7 872-0262-2
The third edition of this groundbreaking book looks at the theoretical foundations of experiential education from a philosophical, historical, psychological, social, and ethical perspective. The articles in this anthology originally appeared in the *Journal of Experiential Education*; they were chosen as the best articles published to address theoretical issues. This new and expanded publication will be an important resource for those new to the field as well as for long-time experiential educators.
AEE Member price $30.00 / Non-member $38.95

EXPERIENTIAL LEARNING IN SCHOOLS AND HIGHER EDUCATION

Richard Kraft and Jim Kielsmeier, editors.
A new edition of *Experiential Education and the Schools*, this updated and expanded anthology contains some of the best articles published in the *Journal of Experiential Education* to address the role of experiential education at all levels of schooling. General theory, service learning, research and evaluation, cultural journalism, the environment, and practical ideas are just some of the subjects covered. This book is a must for educators, school board members, administrators, professors, and researchers who are striving to improve education for all our children, young people, and adults.
AEE Member price $30.00 / Non-member $38.95

**ADVENTURE THERAPY: THERAPEUTIC APPLICATIONS
  OF ADVENTURE PROGRAMMING**
Michael A. Gass, PhD
ISBN #0-8403-8272-3
This valuable resource book contains writings by Dr. Gass and other respected practitioners in the growing field of therapeutic adventure programming. The book's 39 chapters address such issues as why adventure therapy works; programming considerations; the theory of adventure therapy; current research in the field; examples of effective programs; and future directions of the field.
AEE Member price $23.95 / Non-member $29.95

**ETHICAL ISSUES IN EXPERIENTIAL EDUCATION,
  2ND EDITION**
Jasper S. Hunt, Jr.
ISBN #0-8403-9038-6
An examination of the current ethical issues in the field of adventure programming and experiential education. Examples of topics include: ethical theory, informed consent, sexual issues, student rights, environmental concerns, and programming practices. This book encourages experiential education practitioners to reflect carefully on the ethical issues inherent to their profession.
AEE Member price $16.00 / Non-member $23.00

**To order a title call Kendall/Hunt Publishing Company at
(800) 228-0810.**